PRAISE FOR COUNT BINFACE

'There are about twenty jokes on every page. Very funny'

Greg Jenner

'A really funny book, full of great comic ideas and sometimes surprising common sense' **Spectator**

'Our favourite space politician' **Daily Star**

'Count Binface will be Prime Minister. It's only a matter of time' **Independent**

COUNT BINFACE is the intergalactic space warrior and novelty UK politician who has delighted millions with his unlikely tilts at power. First, he took on Theresa May in the 2017 General Election, cunningly disguised as 'Lord Buckethead', and went viral (in a non-Covid way). Then he challenged Boris Johnson in 2019, when he scored 69 votes (he'd love to say he's the first life form to experience a surprising 69 with the former Prime Minister in a sports hall during the small hours, but with Boris you never know). More recently, in 2021 he ran to be Mayor of London in a bid to gain control of the Earth Capital itself, receiving a glorious 92,896 votes that sent him soaring into ninth place. *What On Earth?* is his first book.

COUNT BINFACE

WHAT ON EARTH?

AN ALIEN'S GUIDE
TO FIXING BRITAIN

QUERCUS

First published in Great Britain in 2022 by Quercus Editions Ltd

This paperback published in 2023 by

QUERCUS

Quercus Editions Ltd
Carmelite House
50 Victoria Embankment
London EC4Y 0DZ

An Hachette UK company

A CIP catalogue record for this book is available
from the British Library

PB ISBN 978 1 52943 144 5
Ebook ISBN 978 1 52942 166 8

Every effort has been made to contact copyright holders.
However, the publishers will be glad to rectify in future
editions any inadvertent omissions brought to their attention.

PICTURE CREDITS:
p.37 courtesy of Daniela Shanly, Beech Lodge School; p.42 © Antonio Guillem / Shutterstock;
p.47 courtesy of Mark Amies; p.59 © Kirsty Wigglesworth / AP / Shutterstock

10 9 8 7 6 5 4 3 2 1

Typeset by CC Book Production
Printed and bound in Great Britain by Clays Ltd, Elcograf S.p.A.

Papers used by Quercus are from well-managed forests and other responsible sources.

To Theresa, Boris and Sadiq.
I couldn't have done it without you.

Contents

Acknowledgements

I would like to thank the humans at Quercus[*] for publishing this book. Although I am fluent in over seven million forms of communication, English is not my first language and the original text has been translated from my native tongue. I say this not to apologise for any errors contained in the pages that follow,[†] but to emphasise my total infallibility. In the unlikely event that this volume contains any mistakes or typos, the fault lies squarely with a junior editor named Hugh and I shall see to it that he is dealt with summarily by Vortigua, the Immortal Gravity Beast of Sram.[‡]

I would also like to express gratitude to your planet's so-called 'top 1 per cent'. Messrs Zuckerberg, Bezos, Musk, Trump, Johnson, Bieber et al... I know they are not natural targets for praise. In fact they're amongst the first individuals to have been despised by more than seven billion humans at the same time.[§] However, they have also done something wonderful. It's thanks to the actions of a minority of powerful humans like them that Earth is in an absolute state, and this has opened the door for someone fresh to

---

[*] Which is Latin for 'oak', which is Recyclon for 'knows a good deal when they see one'.

[†] I don't have a tongue, for a start.

[‡] i.e. eaten.

[§] An achievement in itself.

waltz through and seize control, brandishing the most powerful weapons in the cosmos. That someone is me. And those weapons are democracy, lasers and Ceefax.* So to all of humanity's – I believe this is the technical term – mega-bastards, may I offer a hearty thanks for the leg-up.

---

* More on this later. Much more.

Preface

Greetings, life form! Welcome to my book. It is an enormous pleasure to be sharing with you my story, political beliefs and even the occasional recipe, in return for a reasonable – nay, bargain – amount of Earth currency.

If you received this volume as a gift, please congratulate the donor on having such wonderful taste, and yourself for having such an excellent friend. If you bought it personally, you officially belong to an elite vanguard of your species, possessing a level of intelligence that puts you in with a shout of avoiding the twenty-first century's impending catastrophes (well, some of them anyway – the asteroid is going to be hard to miss. Soz). If you found it in a charity shop, it's a pleasure to be joining forces with you in this transaction to raise money for good causes or a donkey sanctuary. If you just happen to be browsing in a bookshop, I suggest you cough up immediately and buy me, or at the very least swap me on the shelves with Richard Osman's latest cosy crimefest so it looks like I'm top of the charts. And if you borrowed it from a library, please don't leave the pages too sticky. The contents are highly potent, but control yourself.

It's a big old omniverse out there, so you might be wondering why I'm choosing to focus my attention on your primitive little world. Well, you've got a healthy publishing industry for one thing, and what's more I've spotted a gap in the market. This volume is the first major contribution from outer space towards shaping the future of Earth, if you don't count the meteor that deep-fried all your dinosaurs a while back. That collision, by the way, was an innocent mistake by my old ancestor Captain VaseHead, who miscued during a drunken game of solar snooker and sent an asteroid plunging smack into your planet's face. I appreciate that an apology for that might be a little bit on the tardy side, but I can relay that VaseHead was truly sorry about it at the time. Then again, his mistake did result in the rise of the mammals and the *Jurassic Park* film franchise, so maybe things worked out for the best. More than anything, what makes Earth special is that over the last 65 million years your planet has given rise to the two rarest and most precious things in all the cosmos. One, antiques-based television drama *Lovejoy**. And two, democracy. And it's the latter I'll be focusing on in this volume. Firstly, because it's in big trouble. And secondly, because I can't do justice to *Lovejoy* in a book of this size. You'll need to download my eight-hundred-hour podcast for that.

There are very few books that can lay claim to changing the course of intergalactic history. *The Insider* by Piers Morgan, *Striker!* by Steve Bruce and *The Devil's Tune* by Iain Duncan Smith are just three examples that had no impact whatsoever. But my book

---

* Antiques-based British television drama starring Ian McShane, and the finest creative endeavour in any art form that Earth has yet produced. I am currently in negotiations with the BBC for the rights to syndicate it on extraterrestrial channels, with a percentage taken on merchandising. Based on the BBC's litany of avoidable mistakes at management level, I'm highly confident of success.

will. In fact, it already has. Somewhere right now an Earthling child (or an Earthlingling, as I call them) is reading this tome and being inspired by it to take up politics and begin their own march to power. Their junior school playground will soon be their, er, playground, and from there control of the galaxy is only a few steps away. That kind of influence is something no self-respecting human would want to be without. So settle down, grab a beverage, and let's make your planet Count.

P.S. Boris, this book won't make sense to you. But give it to Carrie, or Wilf or Romy, or Dilyn, and they'll spoonfeed you the basics.

Part One

**Your Future Prime Minister
and Galactic Overlord**

(Me)

Hello

Allow me to introduce myself.* My name is Count Binface. I am an intergalactic space warrior, leader of the Recyclons, three-time British election veteran, and the Sanest Politician in the Entire Cosmos. That last title is one that's been bestowed upon me by default, owing to the state of all the others, but I'll gladly take it. I hail from a planet called Sigma IX, which is the most 'levelled up' of the Sigma planets by dint of being the least destroyed. If you want to find my home world, just search in the night sky for Orion's Belt, then look due south from there to Orion's flies and head straight through them for about two hours at light speed in your hyper-class starship. Bob's your uncle, BoJo's your dad, that's us. I'm 5,695 Sigmoid years old, which is a good age for a Recyclon because we age like a fine wine, not like an Apple product. My hobbies include invading planets, dominating inferior species and an insatiable desire to binge-watch the *Lovejoy* box set. And my mission is to conquer Earth.

Now, some of the more sceptical members of Britain's political class will be reading my book (and claiming it on expenses) and scoffing at the suggestion they will be vanquished by an eight-foot-tall alien with a bin for a head. But that just goes to show the

---

* That's a rhetorical flourish, by the way. I don't need anyone to let me do anything. For the next 234 pages, I'm in charge.

blinkered, complacent viewpoint of the cosy metropolitan elite. They're all safely ensconced in their Mayfair gentlemen's clubs, sitting happily on Chesterfield sofas and the dreams of the poor, thinking, *is this guy for real?* Well, here it is in black and white: I most certainly am for real. Unlike any of your ludicrous, fictional alien characters like Doctor Who, ALF or Yoda am I. Even if the ability to mangle sentence structures I possess. No, I am an actual alien and I have actual election results to prove it. I have challenged two successive British Prime Ministers to combat at the ballot box, and I am also now officially London's ninth choice to be mayor of the Earth capital, thanks to the 2021 election, when I defeated no fewer than eleven human candidates (including Piers Corbyn* and UKIP).† In that contest I received a total of 92,896‡ votes, which means I was supported by more humans than you can fit inside Wembley Stadium (and that's *after* you count the mob of tanked-up, ticketless England fans breaking through the turnstiles). Not bad for an outsider.

My mayoral result set a new galactic record for the number of votes won by an extraterrestrial in a free and fair democratic election, and it put me second on the official all-time list of most successful non-human politicians on Earth. In doing so I pushed into third place a candidate that went by the name of Pulvapies,

---

* Climate-change-denying lunatic, and brother of Labour Party-destroying lunatic Jeremy. Some of you may think he is from another planet, but sorry guys, he's one of yours.

† The United Kingdom Independence Party. Since Brexit I'm not sure what they want independence from, except their marbles.

‡ Including 24,775 first choice votes. I could tot up the second choice ones but I can't be bothered.

a fungal foot powder who in 1967 ran to be mayor of Picoaza, a small town in Ecuador. To be fair, Pulvapies did win that election, making it the world's most powerful antifungal medication, politically speaking at least. However, according to no less a source than Guinness World Records it garnered 10,000 votes, which is curious considering the town is listed as having a population of 4,000. Something there really stinks, and I'm not talking about the feet.

I'm delighted to have usurped Pulvapies with my current (entirely legitimate) vote tally, but I freely admit there's still a fair way to go for me to catch up with the current non-human record holder. The particular political powerhouse who tops this chart is none other than Macaco Tião, a chimpanzee who ran to be mayor of Rio de Janeiro in 1988 as the candidate of the Brazilian Banana Party. I should add that Tião was a real chimpanzee, as opposed to a man dressed up in one of those novelty costumes you sometimes find. (I can never understand why any human would waste their time mucking about with that kind of idiocy. But with more than seven billion humans on your planet, I guess you're going to get the odd madman.) Tião performed highly creditably in his Rio election, coming third out of twelve candidates and eclipsing my score with a haul of over 400,000 votes. There are a number of lessons that can be drawn from this, such as: one, voters are weird; two, politics in Brazil has gone steeply downhill since the Eighties; and three, I can't yet call myself an unqualified success if I can get resoundingly beaten by a chimp. All those observations are valid but I want you to know I'm hot on Tião's hairy heels and I fully expect to take the undisputed title of Greatest Non-Human Politician on Earth sooner or later. And I certainly don't intend to be as late as Tião, who is dead. For now, the silver medal position will do nicely. It even matches my lid.

So then. How is a receptacle-clad alien proving to be so popular with British voters? Not being Laurence Fox certainly seems to help. But I have also changed the political weather with a series of fresh, sensible pledges like:

No shop to be allowed to sell a croissant for more than £1.

London Bridge to be renamed after Phoebe Waller.

The return of Ceefax, the defunct TV electronic news information service.

And that's just for starters. As you will see in this book, my full manifesto contains a raft of similarly wonderful measures. In fact it's so full of brilliance that you'd need a raft the size of an aircraft carrier to contain them all. An aircraft carrier which, unlike the Royal Navy's, is designed to be able to carry aircraft. Mine is a unique political vision that will transform your life, and mine.

Vision of course is crucial to politics, as the erstwhile Downing Street adviser Dominic Cummings can attest, having claimed that his 2020 lockdown-breaking decision to drive his family to Barnard Castle on his wife's birthday was just an innocent way to test his dodgy eyesight. In the wake of that saga, and with the NHS being so tightly stretched due to repeated government cuts, I wrote to Prime Minister Boris Johnson offering to help Mr Cummings. Using my patented Recyclon technology, I had all the equipment necessary to perform laser surgery on him.

Full disclosure: my aim had been a bit wobbly at the time, so to be on the safe side I took a quick 6,523 light-year trip to the Crab Nebula and back to check if my optical organ was OK and that all went fine (it's a very scenic spot, as it happens – nice for a birthday jaunt). As I explained to Boris in my letter, if I was given the chance to operate on Dom and happened to miss his eyes, zapping his entire brain instead, the operation would have been a complete success. The then Prime Minister didn't reply to my offer but that's understandable. He may have been busy necking a suitcase of wine from Tesco Metro, promoting sex pests and listening to ABBA at the time.

Why Have I Come to Earth?

That's a good question. Which is why I mention it. And it's something I often get asked by my mates on Sigma IX, who wonder why I'm so keen on exploring the omniverse. 'He's been bitten by the travel bug,' they say. And that is true. Once many decades ago I was bitten by a Noxwing, which is a particularly nasty travel bug native to my home world. The wound went bad, and it left me with bin juice seeping out of my lid for weeks. But in terms of explaining my lust for adventure, that's irrelevant. The fact is that I'm an intergalactic space warrior, and if you want to conquer the entire omniverse you can't do it in your bedroom on Zoom. You've got to get out and about and get your digits dirty. I began my career by subduing my planet Sigma IX, followed by the Sigma solar system and the whole Sigma Quadrant. I did it in double-quick time, too. An eminent alien historian who emigrated to Earth used to chronicle similar precocious achievements on your planet. His name was Darth Sidious Waddellious and he noted that 'When Alexander of Macedonia was thirty-three, he cried salt tears because there were no more worlds to conquer. Eric Bristow is only twenty-seven.' Not to brag, I was running an entire supercluster by the age of nine and a half.

I was so successful that pretty soon, as well as controlling more than 900 globes, I had an even more clear-cut sign that I'd made it: my own travelogue documentary series. *Great Spaceway Journeys with Count Binface* is a smash-hit ratings success throughout my quadrant, and although I do own every TV station there, it definitely would have got commissioned anyway. It's a warm, gentle show that's ideal fare for when the suns go down and retired Recyclons are looking for something to numb what's left of their addled brains. In that sense it's very similar to your planet's *Michael Portillo's Railway Journeys* on BBC Two, except that I started mine before the former Conservative MP got in on the act, I annex every place that I visit (Portillo would love to do the same and inwardly seethes that he can't), and unlike him I don't wear ridiculous costumes on camera just to get cheap laughs.

So thanks to my twin motivations of power-lust and generating quality teatime light entertainment, by a tender age I'd already done a lot of travelling and conquering. But I was hungry for more. It's a big old cosmos out there, and even my amazing achievements were just the tip of the iceberg. Incidentally, for future generations of Earthlings who are reading this, icebergs were huge chunks of frozen water that used to populate your planet's poles and oceans, until in the twentieth century humans inexplicably declared war on them. First they tried to kill the icebergs by sailing gigantic cruise ships at them. Then when that failed, they decided to turn the thermostat up on the atmosphere, which has done the trick in terms of pretty much finishing off the icebergs, but with the side-effect of slow-cooking the humans and their habitat at the same time. We Recyclons are just like you in describing such mutually assured destruction as a 'scorched Earth policy'. The difference is that we don't take it literally.

So here's the thing. It's not just that I want to conquer your world. You *need* me to do it, if your future is to be saved (asteroid notwithstanding). And I love Earth.* It's a peculiar, rocky outcrop of a planet, home to more than seven billion humans and countless more interesting species that the humans seem determined to evict. Apart from that it's relatively unspoiled. For alien space tourists it has yet to become a hotspot, although the greenhouse effect is doing its best to change that. Earth's only review to date on StarTripAdvisor reads as follows: 'Went in 1982. Lost my friends. Couldn't phone home. Caught hypothermia by a river and then got experimented on by the locals. Nearly died. Rubbish.' Not exactly a glowing write-up, I'm sure you'll agree. But we can ignore that naysayer, whoever he is. Because the silly fool must have gone

---

* I freely admit that I say this to every species I am in the process of conquering. But with you guys I mean it. (Tbh I also say that bit to every species as well)

to the wrong bit. There's lots here to enjoy. I may be a new boy in these parts but there's no doubt that stumbling across your world has changed my life. And that's no mean feat, speaking as an alien who has done things you wouldn't believe: I've set attack ships on fire off the shoulder of Orion. I've made C-beams glitter in the dark near the Tannhäuser Gate. And I've seen the price of a Jaffa cake in Nicholsons Shopping Centre, Maidenhead. That place really does take the biscuit (or the cake, depending on your Jaffa philosophy).

Start the Count

So how have I ended up as the upcoming political force in this crazy, beautiful and strangely-run place (by which I mean Earth, not Maidenhead. Although the description equally applies). Our story begins in 2017.* I'd been travelling through the Swirly Smear† galaxy on my holidays, as you do, and I was just passing by the Kuiper Belt when my starship – the *Alboreto* – intercepted a number of curious transmissions coming from somewhere in the nearby solar system. The first of them came from a channel called 'UK Gold' and was what I now know well to be an episode of the legendary BBC drama *Lovejoy*. Need I say more? I fell instantly in love with the series, as you

---

* The rest of the omniverse doesn't count time by such an obscure measure as how many times your paltry little rock pootles around your local star. But for the purposes of this book, we'll go with it.

† I believe you call it the Milky Way, which to me just sounds weird.

can imagine, and I reasoned that whatever species conceived of such artistic wonderment must be an advanced civilisation. However, my assumption was immediately challenged by the rest of the transmissions. Taken as a whole, it sounded like a desperate SOS message, containing phrases including: 'Today will go down in history as a dark one for democracy... People in this country have had enough of experts... Nancy Pelosi is on fire... Something you've always wanted to see now on BBC One, Michael McIntyre sings Coldplay.' Whatever planet these messages were emanating from, it was clear to me that living on it must be a species capable of great accomplishments (i.e. *Lovejoy*) and gargantuan piles of rubbish. And rubbish is kinda my thing, so my interest was piqued. Then I heard the most incredible snippet of all: a clip from a news programme announcing that 'the United Kingdom government has called a snap general election', which implied that the country was in dire need of an effective challenger. It seemed that the governing party of this 'United Kingdom' was toying with their own country's future at a moment of national peril by committing an act of idiotic hubris, while at the same time the official opposition was proving to be a complete waste of hyperspace. Whatever they'd done to get themselves into such a pickle, this nation needed something fresh. I leaned back in my comfy captain's chair, tapped my index phalanges together and pondered. 'Those guys are desperate. I'm at a loose end. Why not give it a look, and treat myself to a *Lovejoy* box set while I'm at it?' I told my computer, Barry, to pinpoint the location of the SOS message, which he found to be coming from the third planet in the nearby star system, and the *Alboreto* duly took me there with all speed. That momentous decision changed the course of my ship, my career and my commercial publishing prospects.

It was especially easy for me and Barry to find Earth, because you lot were good enough to send a map. About fifty years ago a bunch of humans called 'NASA' did something your species had never managed before, when they sent a pair of quaint little probes named *Voyager* out into the depths of space. On them they placed a golden disc filled with knowledge, music and a set of directions to your world for aliens to find. Well, we aliens received it all right. So the first thing we knew was that it couldn't have been sent by Hermes. On behalf of all Recyclons, let me express our gratitude for the disc. We analysed its contents, which amounted to a concentrated dose of the very best that humanity had to offer – a polar opposite of *The One Show*. Containing tracks by J. S. Bach, Kamil Jalilov and Chuck Berry, it taught us all about Earthlings' love of baroque, Azerbaijani folk and compilation albums. It was very thoughtful, although a voucher would also have been fine. If I can give some constructive feedback, we didn't need the naked diagrams of human genitalia that NASA also placed on the side of the probe. But that's a small issue, something which the male in the picture also seemed to be suffering from.

It took just a few minutes' hyperdrive travel to reach your planet, and on arrival, I took a moment to gaze upon it from a high orbit. A tiny, fragile, bright blue marble suspended in the infinite blackness of space – is how humans like to think of their world. I'd like to say that your exceptionalism is justified, but honestly, guys, it's not that special. Otherwise you'd probably stop destroying the place. And there are plenty of aliens who'd be repelled by the mere sight of it: blue is the colour of many species' nasal excretions, giving Earth the look of a dried bogey that a Zimloid youngling has spent an entire maths lesson rolling between their fingers into a perfectly spheroid lump. This is just one of many reasons why most aliens give Earth a wide berth.

Luckily I don't have this problem. I emit no nasal excretions because I have no nose.* I stationed the *Alboreto* beyond the dark side of your moon and sent a probe to analyse the United Kingdom and report back on its political status. When I saw the results I would have spat out my coffee, if I'd had any coffee, and if I could spit. The British Earthlings were using none other than a system of democracy! This is a rare thing in the cosmos indeed. It's something we have no need for on Sigma IX, as I have enjoyed untrammelled power as benevolent dictator for the past 9.4 aeons, but I'm delighted to see instances of democracy wherever I find them. Sadly, I could see that your planet's version was under grave threat from powerful forces. Since the 1990s, a succession of complacent leaders had been resting on their laurels, smug in the knowledge that they'd won the Cold War against the Soviet Union. But nobody had told them it was in fact a two-legged fixture, and now they were getting absolutely hammered

---

* This anatomical fact inspired the classic Recyclon gag: 'My dad's got no nose.' 'How does he smell?' 'Via the bionic olfactory implant he was fitted with at birth.' Jokes.

by Russia in the return match. Perhaps I could help illuminate them before it was too late?*

First Impressions

So then. The United Kingdom in the twenty-first century. What a place. As an outsider, what do I immediately think of when I think of the UK? I think manners. I think breakfast tea. I think strawberries and cream. Queuing. Fighting outside pubs. Vomiting in the street. Appalling trains. An infinite quantity of dog excrement. And *Mrs Brown's Boys* (if the last two aren't technically speaking the same thing). No other realm on Earth or indeed the wider cosmos can offer that heady cocktail.

From what I can see, for centuries this was a proud country that built an empire and liked to boast of painting a quarter of the world pink, like some kind of mad, unstoppable Laurence Llewelyn-Bowen. No wonder the rest of the planet trembled in fear. But skipping forwards into the twenty-first century, while Brits' decorating skills remain generally top-notch, the nation's geopolitical sway has atrophied thanks to a series of blunders, whoopsies and untrustworthy decisions by successive governments. Now the only British citizens who can lay claim to a grip over the entire Earth are Ed Sheeran and Mr Bean. The land that boasts the Mother of Parliaments has become an international (and intergalactic) laughing stock, and never more so than since

---

* As we now know, I was too late.

the captaincy of the blond bumshell, Boris Johnson. Once upon a time Britannia ruled the waves. These days she just waives the rules.

The good news is it's not all doom and gloom. Rather, with the future arrival of the asteroid it is going to be doom, but in the meantime it needn't be gloom. There is a chink of light through which the United Kingdom can regain its standing in the world.

My Way In

No sooner had I reached your planet than I made my most important discovery of all, something that would be my portal into Earth politics. It is simply this: the British are deranged. First, they don't even write down the rules to their own system; they just write down what they've done after they've done it, and occasionally check to see if what they want to do next matches up. Second, they let absolutely anyone stand for election. Lining up to challenge the Prime Minister you find all kinds of no-hopers including Howling Lawd Hope, Elmo from Sesame Street and a Liberal Democrat. Whatever that is. Who'd have thought with a system like that you might end up with a lunatic in charge?

I quickly surmised that if I was to make my mark on your planet, the United Kingdom was the place to go. As if I needed any encouragement, even the name of the country was a complete misnomer. In all my days I'd never seen anywhere less united, and for most of the last 200 years it hadn't had a king. And certainly not one called Dom, whatever that strange Mr

Cummings might claim to the contrary. I formed the natural conclusion that power was there for the taking, and made the final preparations for my landing. I wasn't going to the UK just to see the sights or for a few rounds of crazy golf. Well, I was going for that, but not only that. I was in it to win it. Now was an especially timely moment to make my move. From just a cursory look at the state of the nation, it was patently clear that the current generation of human populations had, not to put too fine a point on it, fucked the whole thing up. A dustbin-shaped warlord truly couldn't do any worse.

The Battle of the Magnet Leisure Centre

Time for a quick history lesson. Back in 2017 the British Prime Minister was Theresa May. Remember her? The one who promised 'strong and stable' leadership, and whose idea of fun was to run through a field of wheat? No, I thought as much. She's not very memorable. So we'd better give ourselves a swift refresher. She'd been installed by the Conservative Party as their new leader in summer 2016 after the Brexit referendum, and she began the job by immediately promising to 'build a better Britain'. Even an alien could read between the lines of that. What she meant was, 'I'm hopelessly out of my depth here but I guess I'll have a go at picking through the twisted wreckage left behind by the last guy.' The last guy, I soon discovered, was a gentleman by the name of David Cameron (remember him? No, I thought as much).

Mr Cameron* was the cocky, ham-faced goon who taunted Eurosceptics by calling them 'fruitcakes, loonies and closet racists', only to lose a referendum to the very same nutters and thus recklessly gamble away a nation's security. Humiliated by the defeat, Mr Cameron trotted off the political stage and back to the Cotswolds with his tiny, twirly tail between his legs. Nine months later, speculation was rife that a refreshed government under a new leader might call a snap general election. But a steadfast Mrs May said she wasn't interested in such a cynical gambit, and she kept telling the British public time after time (eight times, in fact) that she wouldn't be going to the polls because she had 'a job to do' and 'it wasn't the time to be playing politics with the country's future'. How very reasonable of her. Then, suddenly, after an Easter walking holiday, she announced a sudden change of heart and decided 'it was the right thing' to dissolve Parliament. Hmm. What could have possibly altered her judgement? Perhaps she had succumbed to temptation on her walk and strayed into a wheat field, slipped on a turd and suffered a terrible blow to her head. Or maybe she'd been seduced by her gigantic opinion poll lead over the Labour Party, which at that point was being helmed by the enigmatic† Mr Corbyn, who was the kind of alternative Prime Minister who made me look like a safe option (which I am). Whatever turned Mrs May's head, her U-turn set an A-bomb under her own premiership, and I resolved to be there to pick up the pieces. I discovered that her parliamentary constituency was

---

* Or 'Dave' to his mates. So let's call him Mr Cameron.
† Enigmatic: (a.) – euphemism for 'fucking useless'.

a curious settlement called Maidenhead, and that all I had to do to seize victory was to convince roughly 30,000 or so humans to vote for me instead of her. Achieve that and I would unseat the British Prime Minister in one fell swoop. Lovely stuff.

Being a newbie, there was something I needed to know before I could make a start on my campaign: what were the basic qualifications required in order to stand for election in the UK? Did you need to have shown competence in politics at a local level, for instance? Did you need a track record in improving the life chances of the community? Did you need to prove that you'd actually lived in the constituency for a few years prior to the election, to demonstrate that you cared about the local area rather than the chance of a leg-up to a cosy career in Westminster? Did you need to be a human being? It turns out you need none of those things. All it takes is 500 quid and ten signatures from local people. It's like they were begging me to do it. I commanded Barry to scour Maidenhead immediately for a discreet place where we could land.

In the meantime, I had some planning to do. Everybody knows first appearances are important, and on this basis I figured that when humans in Maidenhead were deciding who to vote for, some of them might baulk at certain elements of my look, such as the flashing silver of my cloak, the piercing azure blue of my optical visor, or the fact that I have a bin for a face. So I made a cunning tactical move. I decided to adopt a disguise that would help me blend in. Barry analysed the previous 100 years of British electoral history for a suitable camouflage and he discovered that there was a position in high society that had lain vacant for a quarter of an Earth century: the obscure title of 'Lord Buckethead'. This baronetcy had previously been occupied by a little-known figure who had stood in the 1987 election against Margaret Thatcher and then in 1992 against John Major. He had been clad in crude black attire and wore an utterly ridiculous receptacle on his head, yet never uttered a word. He looked like a right idiot. But I spied an opportunity. Could this peculiar defunct aristocrat be my way in?

To begin with, I was curious about who might have been underneath the bucket. Was it an alien like me? Or was it some human joker with too much time on their hands? Playing the system, I secretly lodged freedom of information requests with the British government to discover the identity of this oddball. Intriguingly, the pencil-pushers at Barnet Council did send me a reply, but in it they confessed that they did not know anything about it. This admission in itself was incredible to me. Here was a post-industrialised country with no official record of who had stood on a stage next to two Prime Ministers at crucial points in history dressed like a complete cyberk! But more exciting for me was the discovery that nobody had assumed the mantle of this mysterious figure for the last twenty-five years. Nature abhors a vacuum* and I judged that I'd found the perfect disguise for my visit to Earth. Count Binface running for public office in a general election by posing undercover as Lord Buckethead? It was the last thing they'd be expecting! And so my ingenious plan was hatched: I would take the title, buy a bucket and some junior

---

* Although not as much as it abhors a certain tax-avoiding company that cleans them.

cricket wicket-keeping pads, spray-paint them black and do it my way. That meant not being silent like the previous Buckethead. No way. I would speak, I would sing, I would be political, and above all I would be the best candidate for the job. The scene was set. In June 2017, the Maybot would face a space lord.

Before polling day itself, there was the small matter of convincing some humans to vote for me. That meant hitting the campaign trail. To begin with, I needed the all-important signatures of ten humans from the local constituency to support my candidacy, and even achieving that wasn't a walk in the space park. Knowing that I was bin and shoulders above any other politician on Earth, I sauntered into Maidenhead town centre and visited a number of establishments, asking shopkeepers if they'd kindly sign my form. But, believe it or not, enthusiasm was initially thin on the ground. It didn't seem to matter whether I tried a coffee shop, synagogue or even a dodgy second-hand video games store, everyone looked at me as if I was some kind of bizarre political joke. Were they mistaking me for Mrs May? I didn't see the resemblance.

Fortunately, just in the nick of time I was able to persuade some charming, open-minded Earthlings to back my mission, and at 5 p.m. on Thursday 5 May, the official list of candidates was published on the Internet. And there it was in black and white pixels: 'Buckethead, Lord.' 'May, Theresa Mary.' I'd been accepted into the race. It was game on.

The next thing I needed was a must for any hard-hitting politician: a 'manifesto'. Never having needed to run for election on Sigma IX, this was a new term for me. It is derived from the root words 'manifest', meaning clear, and 'o', meaning nothing whatsoever. But while that's how other parties treated their programmes for government, I saw a chance to stand out from the crowd and embarked on a detailed brainstorming session, to come up with an original set of pledges that would be sure to outflank my rivals. After no less than a full fifteen minutes of thinking, I knew that I'd nailed it. My manifesto was entitled 'Strong (But Not Entirely Stable) Leadership', and it presented a fully costed suite of policies that married fiscal responsibility with a strong interest in lasers. You will find my comprehensive plan for Britain in part five of this book, but for now, suffice to say it included funding for schools, hospitals, social care and other things that humans vote for.

Each pledge was, to use political jargon, a total banger. My full manifesto was the clear market leader and it helped to give me a huge advantage in standing out from rivals (being eight feet tall with a big shiny cape didn't hurt either).

I wondered how long it would take for my campaign to make a mark, but within days I had my answer, in the form of letters from the *Maidenhead Advertiser* and the *Berkshire, Buckinghamshire and Oxfordshire Wildlife Trust*. That's right, I'd caught the attention of the big boys. The *MA* wanted to know if I'd be campaigning inside Maidenhead itself, to which I answered: 'The cloaking device on my ship is malfunctioning and your trains need serious improvement, but if either of these things can be fixed then I may appear. You'll know if I do. I'll be the one with the big bucket on his head.' The BBOWT picked up on this interview and sent me an epistle that asked an important question: 'We note that your spaceship is currently cloaked,' they wrote. 'Could we ask if it is parked in the Maidenhead area? If so, could we politely request that you don't keep it parked on any of the Sites of Special Scientific Interest in the constituency? These sites play an important role in maintaining the terrestrial biodiversity, and our surveyors (who are often using hand lenses) are liable to collide with large, invisible objects, if not suitably forewarned.' Fair enough, but come on guys, I've got to park somewhere. The *Alboreto* is massive, and I'm not paying for an NCP.

Keen to make sure I covered all bases, I followed up my manifesto with another important political weapon: a party political broadcast video. Here was another chance for me to stand out from the crowd, so I used the opportunity to communicate with Earthlings via the majestic medium of song, recording a beautiful cover version of 'Where Are We Now?' by that wondrous alienophile human, David Bowie (if the 'Thin White Duke' were here today, I feel that even he himself would agree my version is definitive). And it was while filming my persuasive serenade, one Saturday morning in May, that I ventured once more into the town centre itself, to greet the locals and introduce myself as (surely) their next MP. Maidenhead seemed to me to be a pleasant location but one that had seen better days. In that sense it reminded me of whenever I have to fly through a meteor shower caused by the destruction of a planet, although I found the Maidenhead one-way system harder to navigate.

The range of humans I spoke to that day was diverse, to say the least. For instance, the first man I met, just outside the town hall, had aviator specs covering his eyes and a large snake draped around his neck. It was an unlikely scene but the man seemed to dig my style (and likewise I his!) and we shared an impromptu fist-bump on the pavement. Already one vote was surely in the can/bucket. As for the snake, I'd never encountered such a specimen before on any world, and I wondered if these slithering, treacherous-looking creatures were native to Maidenhead.

Around the next street corner I found my answer, as I bumped into some canvassers for the UK Independence Party. But what struck me more than anything about this place was how friendly the inhabitants of it were: the kids were beaming, the adults were charming, even the UKIPers were affable (mad, for sure, but very affable). I redoubled my belief that I would be as proud to represent these life forms on the intergalactic stage as they would be lucky to have me.

There was only one individual who displayed any reticence towards me, and that was the Labour Party candidate, Pat McDonald. His team of plucky pamphleteers were a delightful bunch and they seemed keen for me to meet their main man, but Pat himself didn't seem to be quite so up for it. In fact, as soon as he saw me striding towards him for a quick chinwag, he turned on his heels and marched in the opposite direction. It almost looked like he was scared stiff of me, but I didn't want to jump to conclusions – perhaps amid the crowd of morning shoppers he simply hadn't spotted my giant, pitch-black extra-terrestrial frame? Giving him the benefit of the doubt, I followed him down the pedestrianised high street, calling after him, 'Pat! Pat!' until he fled inside the local branch of the hardware store Wilko, not to emerge again until I'd completed my tour of the shops. Some might say that was a bit lily-livered, but I can't fault Pat for his bravery against the odds – he was a foot soldier for Jeremy Corbyn, after all.

As you might expect, by now my campaign was beginning to gather a full head of boiling water vapour, and the media began queuing up to interview me. First there was the local press, then the *NME*, then *Paris Match*, and then finally those slowcoaches at the British Broadcasting Corporation jumped on the bucket-wagon, courtesy of an interview request from BBC Radio Berkshire. Even an extraterrestrial warrior could tell that this was a highly prestigious invitation, so I prepared meticulously to be on top of my brief (and so as not to 'do a Diane').*

Then on the morning of Friday 2 June 2017, my tele-screen bleeped. A key moment had arrived. I was being hailed by the BBC. My inquisitor was a journalist called Linda, and our interview proceeded like none other I have experienced on your planet before or since. Here's a little taste of how it went.

Linda: Have you got any photos from visiting the [local] area?

Me: I will provide you with photographic evidence of my existence in Maidenhead last weekend in due course.

Linda: And are we able to use them? They're not from the *Maidenhead Advertiser* or anything. We're able to use them on the BBC, copyright-wise?

---

* Abbott, mathematically challenged Labour MP for Hackney North.

Me: They were taken by a chap called Giovanni and
           he has given them to me with complete, absolute
           liberty, and I give them to you with the same.

Linda: Oh, amazing! Oh, that's another cherry on the
           cake of today. Thank you very much.

Me: How intriguing. I can tell the sense of a BBC
           journalist because their greatest excitement comes
           from a lack of copyright restrictions. That's very
           telling.

Linda: [Laughs] I'm going to find out who you really are
           one day.

Me: I don't think you are.

Linda: Well maybe after the general election we should
           do a removing of the bin?

Me: That's very flirty.

Linda: [Laughs] Just to see your head.

Me: That's what they all say.

Linda: Well, I'm very glad you've managed to keep up your
           voice for a good ten minutes. I'm very impressed,
           Lord Buckethead.

Me: That almost sounds like a slight level of disbelief
           in this character.

Linda: Well, it's been nice to talk to you.

Me: Well interviewed, well done.

Linda: Thank you!

As you can see, all it took was a bit of political straight talking
mixed with some galactic stardust and I had the BBC wrapped

around my fifth digit (I also avoided talking drivel about being unable to sweat, although in my case that's actually true).

Having conquered the mainstream media, and with a spring in my space-step, I had only one more hurdle to clear before polling day: the tricky task of attending a 'hustings' event* with the humans of Maidenhead. And so, three days before the election, I beamed down from one powerful galactic landmark (the *Alboreto* in orbit) to another (the Oakley Court Hotel, Windsor) to face humanity, and my opponents. But to my disbelief, not a single one of my 'major' rivals showed up! No Mrs May for the Tories. No Pat for Labour. No Liberal Democrat.† Not even the fruitcake and/or loony guy from UKIP.

Instead I took my place on a panel of genial, independent-minded candidates and together we took a grilling from the great and the good, and the grey and the grizzled, of Berkshire. They peppered us with the kind of questions which get lost in the fug of the mainstream media but which mattered to this important local area, like what would I do about the badger population (vaccinate them), the third-party sale of puppies (regulate it) and the redevelopment of the local golf course (hold a consultation). Simples. And then I was asked about the fallout from the 2016

---

* This is a strange word. 'Hustings' are public debates where candidates state their case for being elected in front of their electorate. After a bit of research, using a well-known tax-avoiding search engine, I discovered that it derives from a Germanic word for a governing assembly, called a 'Thing'. There is something particularly appropriate about a forum for British political debate being named after something so wonderfully vague.

+ I'm pretty confident of this, but then again, they so rarely leave a mark it's hard to be 100 per cent sure.

EU Referendum, and I made a proclamation with which I soon became synonymous:

I think I will be able to be more blunt than the politeness of my colleagues allows. And that's part of the reason I am here. Your Prime Minister, your MP, Theresa May, called this election about Brexit. Have we heard from her what she plans to do about Brexit? No. This is mad. On Thursday you are going to be faced with Prime Minister May or Prime Minister Corbyn against twenty-seven Prime Ministers from the European Union. It. Will. Be. A. Shitshow.

Here I was, bringing straight-talking and forward-thinking politics to your solar system, via the conference room of the Oakley Court Hotel. Quite simply, I had a dream: I was going to be the most powerful protest vote in the galaxy, turning Mrs May's safe seat into an ejector seat. All I needed was 30,000 or so humans to agree with me.

Thursday 8 June 2017 was Election Day. Judgement Day. The climactic moment when I would make my bow on Earth's political stage. Well, actually, that's not quite true. Thanks to the quirks and foibles of the British political system, my result would be declared in the small hours of Friday 9 June. So, having arrived in town in the middle of Thursday evening, with the *Alboreto* cunningly cloaked above the car park, I had a few hours to kill.* A space warrior cannot abide time wasted, so I used the opportunity to enjoy the best that the environs had to offer, partaking in the pub quiz at the Maiden's Head[+] pub. Because that's how I roll.

---

* That's in the figurative sense, as opposed to having a few hours in which to do some killing. On Earth I do my fighting at the ballot box.
+ I see what they did there.

Speaking of rolling, I also had time to pop into Desborough Bowling Club for a quick game before joining battle, à la Sir Francis Drake. And to top off a highly pleasant evening, I stopped off for some nourishment at the local Pizza Express.* It was then that the fateful moment arrived for me to take to the electoral battlefield. It was time for Buckethead versus the Maybot. Seconds out. Ding ding.

And where did this intergalactic clash of the titans take place? No less a venue than the Magnet Leisure Centre, Maidenhead. To be hosting a British Prime Minister on the most important night of her political career, not to mention an intergalactic space warrior of some repute, it was no surprise to me that the authorities had chosen what must be one of the nation's most prestigious landmarks. Or at least it was now. A magnet indeed!

In the entrance hall the atmosphere – just like on many a planet that I have subdued – was a curious one. If I were to sum up the vibe, it was somewhere between the Caverns of Praxxi and the Imperial Forum on Vordaniam Beta. Or to translate that into a comparison that humans will understand, my computer Barry tells me that it was like a cross between *House of Cards* and *The Brittas Empire*.† What the Magnet had been lacking was that crucial bit of star power, by which I mean me, rather than nuclear fusion. Everyone was waiting for me to make my entrance. So

---

* Unlike a certain alleged visitor to the Woking branch, I have a receipt and video evidence of my meal to prove it. Not having a digestive system, as such, I am unable to eat per se, so instead I vaporise my food and inhale it gaseously. It's time-consuming and a bit of a pain, but it does at least ensure that everything is cooked.
† I don't know what either of those things are.

amidst huge anticipation, and with a classy swish of my cloak, I entered the fray.*

The central chamber of the venue was a large 'sports hall'. Some might think this a pathetically twee place for a Prime Minister to discover her fate, but it made perfect sense to me, given the sport that was soon to come. The room was teeming with humans, many of them seated at long tables frantically counting the votes, while over to one side were banks of journalists (and Kay Burley) waiting to relay the all-important result to the cosmos. By the door, held back by a cordon, were a cluster of schoolchildren who'd been brought along by their teacher to get a taste of democracy in action. When I entered the hall, every head turned. The journos yelled my name, the kids screamed, and at least one counter lost count of their count (probably). Only one individual was nonplussed by my arrival – a stocky, shaven-headed security guard who shall remain nameless, because I never found out his name. Unlike everyone else swooning at me, this guy clearly hadn't got the memo. That was fair enough, as I hadn't sent him a memo, but he wasn't in the mood to be friendly and (can you believe this?) acted as if my candidacy was some kind of stunt. Far from it. After all, at this election one of the three main parties had a weirdy-beardy leader detested by his own MPs; another of them had a leader who was pleading to implement a highly controversial policy she'd voted against; and the third was led by Tim Farron. I was bringing some much-needed respectability to the

* Not to be confused with the then Conservative MP for Windsor, Adam Afriyie.

race. For the security guard's craven display of insubordination, I briefly thought about lasering the dude, but it wasn't his fault he was ignorant. He was only human.

At 3.15 a.m. Earth time, the returning officer* called everyone to attention at the far end of the hall, and I ascended the stage along with all the other contestants, as I like to call them. I was confident of a swing away from Mrs May towards Buckethead from the last election, for the simple reason that Buckethead didn't stand at the last election. There was only one real question. How big a swing would it be?

In front of an assembled throng at the Magnet, and the eyes of the whole world, my name was called. 'Buckethead, Lord. Independent…' There was a collective intake of 78 per cent nitrogen, 21 per cent oxygen, 0.9 per cent argon and 0.1 per cent other gases.† And then my score was read out: '249'. Two-hundred and forty-nine! A new Buckethead record! More than the previous incumbent of the title had achieved in two elections put together, and a mere 37,469 votes away from being elected. There was only one thing to do. I asked the Animal Rights Party candidate to my left if he could stand back a bit so I didn't accidentally hit him, and then I thrust out my arms to perform a celebratory 'dab', photos of which instantaneously went viral around the planet.

Meanwhile Mrs May looked crestfallen, with the expression of someone sucking on lemons while running through a wheat field.

---

* The returning officer is a kind of political game show host. If the election is *The Chase* then they are the Bradley Walsh of the occasion. It's that glamorous.
† What you call 'breath'.

But then she had just lost her parliamentary majority and fatally damaged her time as Prime Minister. So I could see why she might be a bit miffed. The Maidenhead constituency might be hers, but the moral victory and the zeitgeist were mine. All mine. The Tory leader had been upstaged by a laser-toting, Ceefax-loving space warrior. When you look back, it was pretty much inevitable. But back in 2017 humans were pleasantly surprised that, in the absence of a sane Labour leader, finally someone was speaking truth unto power. As one Twitter user, Nathan McDermott, wrote in reaction to seeing me on stage with Theresa May that special night, 'Truly, democracy is a beautiful thing.' And I was just getting started.

Kicking the Bucket

Thanks to my breakthrough election performance, the hitherto unknown name of 'Lord Buckethead' suddenly resounded around your planet. The *Guardian* voted my Ceefax pledge as the best policy of the whole election campaign, while *The Times* declared that I was 'now the most dominant force in silly costume politics"* and the *Maidenhead Advertiser* garlanded me with their prestigious 'Being of the Year' award.

Within days I was being whisked over to New York City to appear as a special guest star on *Last Week Tonight with John*

---

* This must have come as a shock to that paper's powerful proprietor, who of course resembles a shrivelled scrotal sac with glasses.

Oliver, and as the Alboreto's drive core had overheated, I was flown first class on BA. That raised a few looks among the glitterati and the oligarchs, I'm pleased to say. Back in Britain, I was invited to speak to a crowd of 5,000 people at Glastonbury, the day before Jeremy Corbyn made a similar stump speech at the same festival (he's always one step behind, that dude). Addressing the assembled gathering, I proclaimed that we must hold politicians to account and, above all, when they get things wrong, we must royally steal the urine*. In contrast, Mr Corbyn used his speaking slot to spout that there was a message written at the festival site for Donald Trump: 'Build bridges, not walls.' A noble sentiment indeed, although what the bearded wonder declined to mention was that this message had been written on a wall.

More gratifyingly, I started to receive messages that my tilt for parliamentary power had been having an educational effect, getting students interested in serious politics. Here's a small selection of the kind missives posted on the Internet:

Emily Bell, Professor of Journalism at Columbia University, wrote that my existence 'has enabled me to explain the "first past the post" system to my thirteen-year-old without him passing out through boredom'.

A gentleman named Rob Lewis tweeted: 'Showed my five-year-old Lord Buckethead. His reaction: big pause. Inspired expression. "Wow." Pause. "Cool." Making Plans expression.'

---

* This is a faithful translation of a Recyclon phrase, although I understand that for humans 'take the piss' is more idiomatic and so I used that phrase instead.

A human called Jack reported on his child's behaviour in an American cafe: 'My seven-year-old to a waitress here in San Francisco: "Do you know who Lord Buckethead is? He has his own channel." (Waitress was confused.)'

No greater honour could I receive than when the kids at Beech Lodge School, Maidenhead, performed a mass dab in my honour:

It was a splendid tribute, which I returned by paying a Christmas visit to the school to meet the kids and their wondrous teacher, Daniela.

Meanwhile, someone else put forward this viewpoint: 'There's a British politician named Lord Buckethead??? More like fuckin... lord buttfuckhead.' Oh well. You can't win 'em all. Still, thanks for your feedback, 'Horny Dilbert', whoever you are.

This rare dissenting voice was emblematic of the fact that there's always a flipside to success. Predictably enough, some humans began to pry into my private life and I received several enquiries as to whether there might be a Lady Buckethead. This volume is devoted to my public service in dominating the omniverse, rather than my experiences of romance – unlike some Prime Ministers I could mention, I see the value in not confusing the two. But just to titillate you, there was a Binfacina once. She was a charming Vordavian with a cycloptic robot eye, and we spent many a fun night together on Sigma IX, watching the suns go down and zapping Negworms into space goo. But it all went wrong during a holiday on Phobos, when I discovered she was a double agent for the Oddurms on Sigma X. She never writes, because I sentenced her to eternity in the Phantom Zone. But hey, in this cosmos love is the riskiest gambit of all. For more juicy titbits like that, you'll just have to wait for Book Two.

Meanwhile, as Britain moved into the heights of summer and beyond, so my newfound power on your planet soared to new altitudes. On the BBC, I was privileged to be mentioned by Jonathan Agnew on the *Test Match Special* programme, and I was invited to be the mystery guest during the BBC World Service's 'Quiz of the Year' broadcast (World Service is such a quaint notion – you can't even listen to it on the moon!). As if these bangles and baubles weren't enough, things then kicked up another notch when an effigy of me won the Flamstead Scarecrow Competition, defeating Theresa May* in the process by 102 to 79. Now that's what I call a meaningful vote.

I decided to cap the year by following a favourite British tradition and releasing a festive single, *A Bucketful of Happiness*, because I wanted to pay tribute to my new human fans, and also because I can't resist a good tune. This time I decided to take a cracking melody by the giant musical talent Meat Loaf, and to set it to powerful new lyrics written by yours truly. It may not have reached the Christmas number one slot, but that's only because I'm an alien and I didn't know how to release it. Even so, I did something even better than that, receiving the best review possible from a human parent: 'I managed to get my baby daughter to stop crying for almost four whole minutes thanks to it.' Praise comes no higher than that.

Most gladdeningly of all, throughout my first year on Earth I was inundated with fan mail from all over the globe, including a panoply of photos featuring supporters dressing up as me: adults, children, cats – quite a surprising number of cats, actually. I'm still not sure what to make of that. Taken together, it all amounted to a splendid success. Mrs May may have won the electoral war, but I was the clear victor of the democratic peace, and Maidenhead would always hold a special place in my internal-bodily-fluid-pumping organ. But my honeymoon†

---

* Technically it was a likeness thereof.
† I take it that this is just a phrase, and not a reference to Upsilon IV, a moon in my star system whose surface has the sticky, sickly properties of honey. It's a wonderful place to go for a tasty sweet treat, but the moon is riddled with the rotting hulls of spacecraft that stayed too long and got irretrievably stuck. As with all delicious things, everything in moderation.

period was soon to come to a juddering halt. A storm was coming.

The thing is, everything had gone too well. This is a problem that no British politician has ever complained of before, so I found myself in uncharted territory. But as you humans say, what goes up must come down. Usually I hate that phrase because I spend most of my time in the gravity-free ocean of space and so it doesn't really apply. But on your planet I accept that Sir Isaac Newton was right and for a short while my political dreams were brought crashing back down to Earth.* In February 2018, without fanfare or signal, I disappeared from Earth's political scene. My human supporters wondered where I'd gone. Was I ok? Had I returned to Sigma IX for good? Then on 12 December of that year I dropped my massive bombshell – I had renounced my peerage. I was Lord Buckethead no more.

Why take such a drastic step? Well, I'd pledged to abolish all the Lords in my manifesto and I'm a rare politician who keeps his promises.† So I vacated the Buckethead title and announced myself to planet Earth for a second time, this time respawning in my true guise as Count Binface. I'm not going to lie, it felt

---

* As indeed did the *Alboreto*, which I had to emergency land in the Thames Estuary after a steering issue. Fortunately the ship was cloaked at the time so nobody saw, and I definitely didn't graze the Palace of Westminster's 'Big Ben' tower on the way through.

† There was also the small matter of an unfortunate battle on the planet Copyright. Plenty of juicy details remain to be revealed about this, but I'm happy to wait to tell you about it until I become an MP, when I shall be protected by parliamentary privilege to say whatever I want (yet another good reason to vote for me).

great. In yet another historic first, I was the first politician in the entire omniverse to feel better after kicking the bucket. It was time to rise again.

Unshackled from the bucket, I was now free, stronger, and with a newfound appreciation of brands such as WWE, Boss Cat and AFC Wimbledon.* I could feel that karma was on my side, and so too, I soon discovered, was the great nation of France. Within days of outing myself as Binface, I was invited to take part in a special Brexit-themed documentary for French television presented by the mighty Antoine de Caunes of *Eurotrash* fame. Of course I readily agreed. *La langue de la poubelle est ma langue naturelle.* Trash is my language. So Antoine and I got on like *une maison en feu.*

The location for our interview was a dank King's Cross pub, which was my kind of place. If anything, it could have been danker. As we sat down for a pint of Earth ale on a freezing winter's morning at 9 a.m. – those Frenchies seem to be hard drinkers – and enjoyed a quaint game of 2D pool, I allowed myself a moment to take stock of the situation. Here I was, being interviewed by the co-presenter of a late-night cult entertainment show on Britain's fourth TV channel in the mid-1990s. There was only one conclusion that could possibly be drawn: I was back.

---

* Renaming can be a tricky gambit on any planet.

A human fan sums things up nicely through the medium of meme.

A New Opponent

It's no exaggeration to say that, after my skirmish with her in 2017, Mrs May's government was mortally wounded. Whatever political stripe you are, I think we can all agree on that. Having unencumbered herself from her parliamentary majority and any vestige of authority, her final defenestration was only a matter of time. So it's to her immense credit that she clung onto the door frame of Downing Street for another two orbits of your sun, especially after her performance at the 2017 Conservative Party Conference. That's the one where she was assailed by a prankster waving a P45, and suffered the indignity of seeing even the Tory slogan fall apart, as the F in 'Building a Country that Works for

Everyone' dropped off the wall behind her and onto the floor (a literal F-Off in front of millions). Most memorably of all, Mrs May had contrived to be struck down by a nasty cough on the day of the speech, causing her to barely be able to say a word and eventually provoking the then Chancellor of the Exchequer to hand her a throat sweet. It has gone down as one of the most excruciating conference speeches ever delivered,* but I should point out that a muffled voice is not always a barrier to success. As if to sum up the hapless dying embers of the May premiership, the PM was forced into a corner over the question of how she would vote if there was a second Brexit referendum. 'I don't answer hypothetical questions,' was her queasy reply. If only a single journalist had thought to ask the obvious follow-up: 'But what if you did?'

While the sad end of the Maybot was eminently predictable, what was surprising to me – and yet seemed tragically inevitable for humans – was that the Conservative Party chose to replace trembly Theresa with somebody even less fit for office. And not just anyone. That's right, dear reader, we have arrived at the era of the blond bumshell† himself, Boris Johnson. If you ask me, this character is a deeply implausible politician with a ludicrous image, clearly unfit for high ministerial office. It's a shame it took Tory MPs many years and many, *many* scandals to twig this simple truth. But those guys are always a bit slow on the uptake.

There are many aspects of this absurd human that are clouded

---

* Give or take the entire oeuvre of Nigel Farage.

† Note to editors: can an alien copyright this phrase? I think it could be the next 'omnishambles'.

in mystery. How anyone has ever believed a single word that's
come out of his mouth, for example. One thing that we know
for certain is that within hours of taking office, according to the
science of human gestation, Mr Johnson was celebrating carnally,
because precisely nine months later he became a father for the
____th time.* The timing is curious because his ascent to the post
of Prime Minister was an event which every other human on
the planet was struggling to conceive. In due course Mr Johnson
proceeded to call his new son Wilfred. I assume this is because he
names his children alphabetically in the same way that the Met
Office does with storms. It may be that Mr Johnson's fondness
for reproduction is an attempt to do his bit to increase Britain's
population, in order to compensate for the workforce issues inevitably caused by Brexit. The numbers won't be precisely equivalent,
but they may be surprisingly close.

It didn't take long for Boris to start exploding the bedrocks
upon which one of the world's oldest democracies was built.
Within weeks, he had illegally prorogued the British Parliament,
causing outrage among thousands of people who couldn't believe
he'd stoop so low, and confusion among millions more who'd
never heard of the word 'prorogue'. But Bojo was just warming
up, and within months he was sending voters to the polls in yet
another general election in December 2019, calling it a 'once in
a generation election'. Indeed, it was the second once-in-a-gener-
ation election in the last three years. His plan was to capitalise on

---

* Please fill in the gap when this detail becomes known. I suggest using a light
pencil.

a parliamentary stalemate with the campaign slogan 'Get Brexit Done'. With an inane smirk on his face, Mr Johnson assured the public that it was possible for Britain to have its cake and eat it. What he neglected to mention was that the cake he was offering was made out of pure human excrement.* These developments condemned the UK to becoming the laughing stock of the solar system, but for me it was all music to my auditory sense organ. For decades, no human politician (or law enforcement officer) had seemed able to lay a glove on this bizarre blimp of a man, as he sailed through controversies in journalism, the London mayoralty and on a zip line. Now opening up before me was a prime opportunity to show the galaxy that for some jobs you really need a specialist. I punched the coordinates into my navicomputer and headed straight to his constituency of Uxbridge & South Ruislip. Destiny was calling me again.

The Battle of Brunel University Sports Centre

The date was Friday 13 December 2019. The time was 3.24 a.m. The weather was heavy rain with a chance of snow, and your strange little world was drawing to it eyes and ears from across hyperspace.† Space armies dropped their weapons; workers downed their tools; lovers became more aroused. The attention of the whole cosmos was fixed on the western edge of the Earth

---

* One day I intend him to keep his word and eat it.
† To be fair, some intelligent species do not possess either eyes or ears, but I assure you they were equally transfixed by the occasion.

capital London, on a lowly sports hall in Hillingdon, and more
particularly on me. Just the mere anticipation of the event was
creating a shockwave so gigantic, its ripples would knock comets
off their orbit. The time had come for my second battle with a
British Prime Minister: Binface vs Boris. The omniverse was on
tenterlasers to see how I'd done.

By this point in time, it was apparent that Boris Johnson's
Conservative Party had won the British general election.[*] But
that detail was merely incidental. Far more relevant was the fact
that right now Mr Johnson's own political future was less secure.
Would the blond bumshell retain his parliamentary seat and thus
his job? Or would he lose out to his charismatic cosmic challenger? Here we were, a part-time novelty politician with a crazy
manifesto and trademark ridiculous item on top of his head, and
me. Two statesmen from two planets, brought together by the
wonder of democracy to a rickety stage in a university leisure
centre, our fates entwined. Unlike most of the statistics that ema-
nate from Mr Johnson, you couldn't make it up.

Election night was the culmination of four weeks of ploughing
the campaign trail, as Mr Johnson and I grappled for control of the
territory of Uxbridge (and South Ruislip), and boy did the battle get
juicy. Being an intergalactic traveller who had set foot in the constituency on precisely two occasions, I had the advantage of knowing
the area better than Boris. And despite the Tory leader's mammoth
PR machine I matched him stride for stride. I was standing on the
same platform as 2017 – not literally, I assume that one is still in

---

[*] Yes, really. Take that in for a moment.

Maidenhead – but enhanced with new, bold pledges that the Tories couldn't match: such as 20,001 new police officers, £1 trillion per week for the NHS, and making Piers Morgan zero emissions by 2030. Showing my intimate knowledge of the local area, I promised to move the hand-dryer by the urinals at the Crown & Treaty pub to a more sensible position:

You see. It's scandalous. And just to make sure that my optimistic vision for Britain wasn't outstripped by the fantasy comic book that was the Labour manifesto, I promised to throw in free broadband for everyone too. Meanwhile my tentpole policies from 2017 were continuing to gain traction, and across a wider swathe of the nation than ever before:

Jess Phillips Esq., ✅
@jessphillips

Count Bin Face's policy of keeping
Ceefax was actually raised with me
today in Yardley, perhaps he's on to
something.

23:21 · 04/12/2019 · Twitter for Android

Even so, as with any campaign (if you're choosing not to deploy the might of your fully armed battle fleet), not everything went precisely as I would have liked. This time I was faced with a uniquely bizarre problem: some humanoids decided to stand in the same constituency in my previous guise of 'Lord Buckethead'! Why would they do that? Was there a possible whiff of skulduggery going on under the bucket? You might think that. I couldn't possibly comment. It was highly confusing for voters, a number of whom told me afterwards that they'd voted for the doppelbucket assuming that it was me. But the craziest fact was that this time, at a general election, I was taking on not only the British Prime Minister but also effectively myself. I'm going to stick my neck out and say that this was unprecedented, on Earth or any planet.

Dramatic and journalistically interesting though my tussle with the doppelbucket was, my focus for the 2019 campaign was again trained, laser-like, on the main parties. Mr Johnson spent his time spouting the notion that his Brexit deal was 'oven-ready', when quite clearly it was shop-soiled, past its sell-by date and a hazard to public health. This election was taking place when the Covid pandemic was just a glint in a diseased bat's eye, and years before he would go on to lie to Parliament about parties inside 10 Downing Street, as well as a host of other misdeeds that eventually and inevitably did for him.

Even though many of his most outrageous transgressions were as yet unknown, you didn't need to be a rocket surgeon to know that he was a sliiiiiightly dodgy choice for PM. As I told the public via an exclusive interview with the *i* newspaper, his relationship with the truth was so elastic you could put it in a bodysuit and call it Mrs Incredible. It was unfathomable to me that no human inside the Conservative Party or the opposition had yet been able to stop his bizarre rise to the top. But that's where Count Binface came in: finally there was someone on Earth who had come to take out the trash.

The local hustings event was the perfect chance to do that. Or so I thought. For this night of oratorical jousting, the humans had once again chosen an important landmark – the bright lights of Yiewsley Baptist Church, West Drayton. It gets no bigger than that (I assume). But while the Labour candidate, Ali Milani, did show up to trade philosophical blows, Mr Johnson was highly notable by his absence (as was the doppelbucket). The three independent candidates who were present, including myself, were given the opportunity by the organisers to draw lots to see who would take Mr Johnson's place on the platform, and with the power of destiny behind me, I won the chance to state my case for conquering Uxbridge (and South Ruislip). It was time well spent: over the course of two hours I stated my support for more cash machines in north-west London, for pro-democracy protestors in Hong Kong, and for turning down the central heating in Yiewsley Baptist Church. It was enough for one voter to tell the assembled gathering, 'I feel like I've entered a slightly parallel universe here this evening, to be fair, when the most credible candidate seems to be Count Binface.' Thunderous*

---

* If you imagine the sound of thunder that is roughly twenty miles away.

applause followed. As if that wasn't enough, by 10.30 p.m. that night, I was the lead item on BBC London News. The information war was tipping my way. And/or it was a slow news day.

And that brings us back to election night itself. There was a long wait for the results announcement, which was unsurprising as Brunel University Sports Hall was being used as some kind of hub venue, where not one but three separate constituencies were being counted: it was the electoral equivalent of a multiplex cinema, just with fewer nachos. At Maidenhead 2017 I'd travelled alone, but this time I was accompanied by my Recyclon strategists, Eiye and Beeye, whose impossible beauty complemented my own and immediately drew the gaze of the world's press. Together we used the waiting time to mingle with a wide assortment of humans and see what made them tick. I listened patiently as a slumped-shouldered Liberal Democrat[*] bemoaned her party's ludicrous Brexit policy to an alien with a bin for a head; I exchanged pleasantries with newscasting legend Andrew Marr, telling him how much I loved his own red planet which neighbours Earth; I observed Labour's deputy leader John McDonnell, as the crestfallen economic fantasist awaited the result for his Hayes and Harlington seat, and reality dawned on him that the Reds had handed carte blanche to the blond bumshell; and I even chatted to a curious, middle-aged gentleman who had turned up to the count looking like a nightmarish clown figure. It wasn't Boris, I must emphasise. This was someone else, clad in multi-coloured garb and hideous make-up. 'Why are you dressed like that?' I asked. 'No reason,' he replied. That's humans for you.

---

[*] I still wasn't sure what one of these actually was.

At the count with my Recyclon strategists, Eiye and Beeye.

Comparing swingometers with Andrew Marr.

The crunch moment came just after 4 a.m. Into the hall swept a vast Conservative column,* headed by Bojo and flanked by his two most trusted advisers, then-fiancée Carrie Symonds and Dilyn the dog (in no particular order). Just like in Maidenhead two Earth years earlier, I was summoned by the returning officer (a lovely chap called Lloyd) to gather in a circle with my fellow contestants, to be readied for the results declaration. At this point the constituency's two principal candidates found themselves for the very first time standing next to each other, face to Binface: Mr Johnson, in the blue corner, representing the Conservative Party; and me, not put in any corner, baby, representing the omniverse. This was it. I'd been waiting for this, Boris. We meet at last. The tension was palpable. I'd say there was an electricity filling the air, but that would send the 5G conspiracy nuts into meltdown so let's just say it was exciting.

How you approach a key moment like this is critical. Our political daggers might have been drawn for the last month but Recyclons know that it's always important to retain a sense of decorum, no matter the gravity of the occasion.† After all, even wars can be civil. Being fluent in over seven million forms of communication,‡ I decided to grab the initiative and to break the ice by greeting Boris, doing so in the only way I felt sure he'd understand: ancient Latin. So I turned to face him and proclaimed a greeting:

---

* A serviceable euphemism for Mr Johnson himself
† In my experience, the lower a planet's gravity, the less chance of retaining decorum.
‡ I know I told you this in the preface, but some droids who can speak a million fewer dialects never stop banging on about their skills so I reckon it's worth at least a second mention.

'*Salve*, Prime Minister!'*

At this stage he seemed reluctant to make eye contact, but even so he merrily agreed with my sentiment, flashing a smile and responding doubly: '*Salve. Salve.*'

Excellent. First contact had been established. I took the chance to peer down at the childlike scrawl of notes that the Tory leader was clutching for his imminent post-results speech and I tried to decipher the words contained on the page. Curiously I then noticed that Boris was doing the same. I've heard it said that Boris is not a details man. If this was anything to go by, he wasn't too hot at the broad brushstrokes either. Honestly, the man's hand-writing was less proficient than a doctor on a rollercoaster. As the then PM squinted at his scrap of paper, he was interrupted by a bystander who called out, 'Are you going to get Brexit done now, Boris?' I pounced upon the opportunity and translated the question into Latin to help the PM understand, quoting the mighty Earth leader Julius Caesar:

'*Alea iacta est*,† Prime Minister?' I asked him.

At this Mr Johnson softened. He cracked a wider smile and again repeated back to me the phrase I'd said to him – *alea iacta est* – showing that he was capable of basic cognitive function. As he did so, his voice was laced with a mix of satisfaction and understandable disbelief, and he looked up at me, blinking his beady eyes. Boris is often accused of dissembling‡, but right now

---

* 'Hello.'

† 'The die is cast,' as Caesar said on crossing the Rubicon, his point of no return on the road to taking power in Rome.

‡ Which is fair enough; he's a liar.

there was no mistaking the thought that was going through the mind of one of Earth's most powerful men: 'This intergalactic space warrior knows his Latin.'

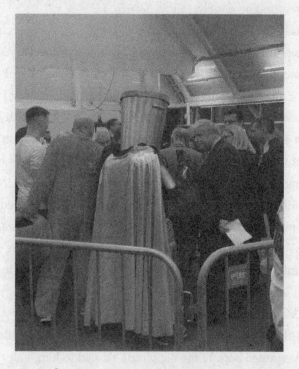

Now that Mr Johnson had reached the conclusion that the two of us were on a level,* we engaged in a smattering of small talk. I told him about what I'd been up to since the 2017 election, including my recent unfortunate battle on the planet Copyright. 'Oh my goodness. Really? Is that so?' the Prime Minister said, with the same caring sincerity he tends to deploy when feigning

---

* As if.

interest about underfunded public services. I must admit I was slightly touched by his forced sympathy, which is something I've also had to master for when Recyclons bother me about a new crater that's appeared on their local hyper-road. But there was no time to dwell on emotion tonight. Lloyd had called us to order.

There was now just one formality to be gone through until we received our verdicts from the good humans of Uxbridge (and South Ruislip). It was up to Lloyd to carry out the traditional ritual of announcing to the circle of assembled candidates the details of any spoiled ballots in this constituency. For anyone not au fait with spoiled ballots, these little beauties are what results when a citizen bothers to turn up at the polling station on election day, but instead of writing an X in a single candidate's box, they decide to go off the beaten track with their marking and to do something more exotic. I appreciate this phenomenon far more than the worryingly prevalent act of not voting at all: it's OK, Earthlings, *Homes Under the Hammer* will still be there on iPlayer when you get back from the church hall. You can do both! Sometimes a spoiled ballot can be the result of sheer idiocy on the part of a voter, but in many cases it is a deliberate protest, and on the odd occasion it can involve a display of unusual creativity. The former Conservative MP Heidi Allen has told me how at one election a voter drew a human penis in her box, and another one for the rival Liberal Democrat candidate. However, because Heidi's phallus was flaccid and the Lib Dems' was erect, it was decided that her opponent should get the vote, on the basis that it seemed the more purposeful. And to think that Lib Dems are the ones who tend to be thought of as too soft. For any Briton who shares this artistic voter's view, and considers profane art to be more worthwhile than electorally supporting any of the main parties, I hear you, guys. Indeed, in the hope of hoovering up support amongst the penis-sketching community, I would like to think that a vote for me is a spoiled ballot with a touch of galactic flair. If you believe conventional politicians are dicks, make your vote Count!*

Tonight there were no such illustrations to be admired, but Lloyd took me and the other candidates through the variety of ballots that certain voters from Uxbridge (and South Ruislip) had chosen to spoil on this occasion. Several had an X in more than one box and so had to be discarded as void, while a few had been left completely blank, which seemed like a missed opportunity to me. Then Lloyd paused, coughed and announced with quiet authority that, 'The next one has been marked, but not with an X. This voter has written across the page the phrase, "C*** Boris".'

Lloyd then held up the ballot to prove it† and many humans around me started sniggering. From one CB to another, I sympathised with Mr Johnson. Sadly, amid the ensuing laughter, I was unable to decipher whether this ballot had counted as a vote *for* Boris or against him. Still, no matter. The crucial news was

---

* I have an idea for a TV documentary series for your planet, in which I detail the most amazing examples of this bizarre art form. It's called *Canvass on Canvas*. Netflix, drop me a line.

† By which I mean to demonstrate the existence of the statement, rather than to prove its veracity.

still to come, and I was more confident than ever that history was beckoning me. Lloyd reached the end of the spoiled ballots and ushered us to the platform for the results announcement. At last! Earth's finest ever playwright William Shakespeare once wrote that 'all the world's a stage'. Well right now, mate, the whole cosmos was. Brunel University Sports Hall was the centre of the galaxy and beyond.

We filed onto the stage and I positioned myself to Boris's left, where, as with his politics, there was plenty of space. In front of us was a sea of cameras and reporters and, ever the professional, I took a moment to wave to the two most important outlets, the *Uxbridge Gazette* and *Sigma Quadrant News*. But then to business. Among the menagerie of twelve candidates on offer to voters I was the first and foremost, both galactically and alphabetically, so my result would be the first to be read out. Lloyd took to the podium and began the customary results announcement, following centuries of Earthly tradition. My spinal implants tingled.

'As the returning officer for the constituency of Uxbridge (and South Ruislip), I do hereby declare that the number of votes cast is as follows.'

Come on, Lloyd. Hit me with it.

'Count Binface, Independent… sixty-nine.'

A hush swept through the hall, and my mind did space-cartwheels as I tried to take this news in. Then a cheer erupted. SIXTY-NINE. The magic number. Recyclons are not naturally superstitious but we believe that sixty-nine has magical properties, capable of bestowing mutual joy to multiple individuals at the same time. How the space gods were smiling upon me. On this night of all nights, I had just experienced a sixty-nine with Boris Johnson in a London sports hall at 4 a.m. on Friday the thirteenth under a full moon (I'd love to say that this was a first, but of course with Boris you never know). Still, what a climax.

As a small sidenote, Lloyd proceeded to announce that Mr Johnson had won the constituency with a majority of 7,210. Some might say that my total was a mere pinprick on the tough, leathery hide of the monster that is the Tory Party, but that would be to concentrate only on the facts. The headline news was that my thrilling sixty-nine represented a massive 0.1 per cent swing away from the Conservatives to Count Binface.[*] A blow had been struck. As I write this now, I owe a debt[†] to each and every one of those brave Uxbridgians (and South Ruislipites) who voted for me, and gratitude to them continues to fill my internal fluid-pumping organ. I celebrated on the stage by performing my customary dab, while my opponents chuntered in disillusionment as they realised the limelight had been stolen. Journalists began filing stories, and these started pinging around the Earth's internet and far beyond, spreading news of my success. Most wondrously of all, the *Washington Post*, the newspaper famed for exposing the Watergate scandal, printed the following photo:

---

[*] #swingbin.
[†] This is a metaphor, not a promise of hard currency.

The caption underneath the picture read 'British Prime Minister Boris Johnson, left.' It was a truth universally acknowledged. Reader, I bested him.

A Capital Idea

In the wake of my historic campaign in Uxbridge (and South Ruislip), I hyper-jumped home to Sigma IX for some much-needed R 'n' R.* Meanwhile back on Earth, on 31 January 2020 the newly emboldened Boris Johnson got his way and officially pulled the United Kingdom out of the European Union. Completely unrelated to these twin harbingers of doom, within a matter of days the entire country was struck by a deadly pestilence, with the arrival of the Covid-19 pandemic on British shores. As you'll know, unless you spend your life under a rock or you are Gavin Williamson, this turned life on your planet upside down. And

---

* Rest and Relining.

one of its important side effects was to postpone the election to decide who should be the next mayor of London.

The contest was thus rearranged for 6 May 2021, and that brings our story back to where we started. Owing to the fact that my government on Sigma IX is infallible and everything there is completely tickety-boo,* I had a gap in my schedule at just the right moment and so I sped my way back to your solar system. After my previous campaigns in Maidenhead and Uxbridge (and South Ruislip), it was the natural next step to challenge for power over the entire Earth capital itself. With the role having been previously filled by Boris Johnson and Ken Livingstone, I figured that voters might be ready for someone serious for a change. What with Covid being what it was, the official advice for interstellar space warriors was to maintain a distance of at least one planet from Earth at all times. Even though I was an early adopter on the face-mask front, I was happy to heed this warning and so I set up a battle base on Mars and opted to run an entirely digital campaign. It was to be my greatest triumph yet, which I launched with the catchy imprecation: May the Sixth Be with You.

To woo votes from the inhabitants of this mighty city, I knew I needed even more policy firepower and this inspired me to cook up a new, highly potent manifesto that completely wrong-footed every other candidate. No human standing came anywhere close to offering my wondrous pledges, which comprised a twenty-one-point plan for 2021:

---

* You'll just have to take my word for that. Unlike Vladimir Putin I will never ban foreign media from reporting on my regime. But for some reason you guys haven't sent any cameras or reporters. Your bad.

- London Bridge to be renamed after Phoebe Waller.
- Hammersmith Bridge to be repaired, and renamed Wayne after the former England international footballer.
- Croydon to get a facelift, ironically.
- No shop to be allowed to sell a croissant for more than £1.
- Free parking between Vine Street and the Strand (for electric vehicles only).
- HS2 protestors to be allowed to build their tunnel at Euston, all the way to Birmingham. To be followed by a second tunnel that links Birmingham to Manchester.
- Finish Crossrail.*
- At Trafalgar Square, Sir David Attenborough to be placed on the fourth plinth. Or a statue of him. Either's fine.
- Speaker phones on public transport to be banned. Offenders to be forced to watch the movie version of *Cats* every day for a year.
- London to join the EU.
- All government ministers' pay, including the mayor's, to be tied to that of nurses for the next 100 years.
- Loud snacks to be banned from theatres.
- The Trocadero to be turned back into a truly top-notch video arcade.
- Piers Corbyn to be banished to the Phantom Zone.
- I will create a Smart Speakers' Corner, replacing the usual nutters who stand around Hyde Park with state-of-the-art

---

* Belatedly, human politicians have copied this policy and got it done, but I'm claiming it as a win.

technology that (a) understands the Earth is round, and (b) will perform a fart sound on command. The current incumbents can only do the latter.

- On one day every year, escalators on the Underground to be reversed, encouraging travellers to go up the down escalators and down the up ones, as a free gym and *Gladiators* simulator all in one.

- Mask wearing in public to be encouraged, during the pandemic and beyond.

- The royal family to keep one of Buckingham Palace, Kensington Palace, St James's Palace and Clarence House, with the rest gifted to the nation to help eradicate homelessness. If the royals complain that one palace isn't enough, they will be forced to buy Crystal Palace FC.

- The hand-dryer in the gents' toilet at the Crown & Treaty, Uxbridge, to be moved to a more sensible position.

- Traitors' Gate to be reopened for business, and to welcome Dido Harding on Day One.

- Ceefax to be brought back for all households within the M25.

It was my greatest suite of policies to date. Within the blink of a lid-protected optical organ, I was trending across social media, as were 'Ceefax' and 'Trocadero' – about time. I also soon hoovered up support from a powerful coalition of Earth-based celebrities, who were all joining forces to make their vote Count:

'*Now this – THIS – is a proper manifesto. Point 19 is clearly urgent, and all candidates should adopt it.*' (Jay Rayner)

'*I have to be honest, I agree with almost every policy in this manifesto.*' (Professor Brian Cox)

'*@profbriancox I hear you xx.*' (Lorraine Kelly)*

'*#VoteBinface on the strength of point 18 alone.*' (Jack Monroe)

'*No one can beat this. Proper policies that will make a lasting difference in London.*' (Omid Djalili)

'*Vote Count Binface – particularly as the preferred option.*' (Sir Matthew Pinsent)

'*Best [manifesto] I've seen yet.*' (Gary Lineker)

It wasn't just individuals who were drawn to the might of the Bin. There were institutions too. First the Hawksmoor steak restaurant promised not only to support me but also to thoughtfully position the hand-dryers in their public toilets; then I was highly flattered to receive approval from none other than the 'Dorset Independence Party' – now, my geography of Britain is admittedly a little hazy, but I assumed that it must be useful to win

---

* Anyone on Earth who doesn't know who Lorraine is must be a vapid individual indeed.

support from the London Borough of Dorset. Otherwise, why were they getting in touch? (They'd have to be a right bunch of crazies.) More importantly, once again I was proving to be a big hit with future voters, with more than one human getting in touch to tell me that their younglings had been inspired by my intergalactic example and created a manifesto of their own. For instance, the ten-year-old daughter of a gentleman called Craig had some cracking ideas, such as:

- Wednesdays off school (because the food is yucky).
- No more climate change.
- Lock Donald Trump in the chokey.
- Don't get drunk.
- If you prick your finger five times in one sewing session, go and buy a pet crab.

A career as a special adviser is surely in the offing. Likewise a six-and-a-half-year-old girl called Marianna sent me some frankly banging ideas like these:

- Ban all spicy candles.
- Give houses to homeless people for free.
- Make everyone eat fruit at least three times a day.
- Don't teach scary things to children.
- Put Donald Trump in prison.

While every child's imagination is unique, at least one consistent theme was emerging: Mr Trump has got a bad rep with the kids.

In fact, let's briefly turn our visors towards Mr Trump. This orange monstrosity's elevation to the White House was a singular event that changed forever the history of the American presidency. For instance, an astonishing new truth about John F. Kennedy is that after the events in Dallas on 22 November 1963, the thirty-fifth President still had more brains than the forty-fifth one possessed on taking office in 2017. The United States traditionally likes to see itself as the leader of the free world and, according to many commentators, during the Trump years that proud country abdicated its awesome responsibility. This is unfair. I would argue that by being free enough to elect as head of state such a toxic, dangerous imbecile, the US proved it was not just a world leader but a galactic frontrunner too. If his four years in office felt to you like they lasted a lot longer than that, then you'd be right. It will have felt like that. The man is so dense that he actually warps the spacetime around him.

But enough about him. Back to my 2021 mayoral race. I needed to keep my focus on the Earth capital, not least because there were no fewer than *twenty* candidates vying for the throne. As a ruthless Recyclon space warrior I stood out a bit, because among this company I was one of the saner choices. Up against me was a right smorgasbord of no-hopers: there were anti-vax 5G loonies, a Liberal Democrat, UKIP's delightfully named Peter Gammons, and an American who crowed about drinking his own urine. In 2019 I'd met my fair share of novelty candidates taking the piss, but this stuff was off the charts.

Among the herd of eccentric opponents, it's fair to say that a couple should be singled out. First I must highlight Piers Corbyn, a man who has achieved the impossible in making his brother Jeremy look like a safe pair of hands. With the benefit of my interstellar objectivity, it was clear to me that Piers's dangerous views about the Covid pandemic needed dealing with, hence my policy pledge to banish him to the Phantom Zone for an eternity of infernal punishment. But to be fair to him, this didn't stop his campaign team from inviting me out on Good Friday for an Easter demonstration against what he called 'BBC psyops'. Keen to maintain a sense of decorum among the candidates, I sent Piers this reply:

Thanks for the invitation. Please accept my apologies but I won't be attending Piers Corbyn's rally on Good Friday. Even space warriors running for mayor like to put their feet up on a bank holiday, and ranting at the treasured, embattled national broadcaster in the middle of a pandemic is not really my idea of fun. Plus I don't want to miss Carry On Doctor on ITV3. I hope you have a peaceful demonstration and I look forward to hearing all about it… on BBC News.

Galactic best wishes,

CB x

Mr Corbyn may have been a loopy fly in the ointment of sanity, but in the grand scheme of things he was just a sideshow. The media decided that the real battle royal in this election lay elsewhere, between me and controversial actor Laurence 'Lozza' Fox, who was running as the candidate for 'Reclaim' (pronounced: 'Reek, Lame'). In particular, a lot of press attention greeted this statistic:

Count Binface
@CountBinface

ELECTION CAMPAIGN **BUDGET**:
Laurence Fox: £5million
Count Binface: Zero

LATEST POLLING:
Laurence Fox: 1%
Count Binface: 1%

#MakeYourVoteCount

11:42 · 21/04/2021 · TweetDeck

ılı View Tweet activity

6,018 Retweets **557** Quote Tweets **42.1K** Likes

A quick word about Mr Fox. He was widely pilloried for his inflammatory views, but I had a hunch that this revulsion is unfair. Analysing his performance at close quarters, I developed an alternative theory. As I told ITV News, surely nobody – not even a human – could possibly believe some of the claptrap that Lozza was coming out with. So, I thought, perhaps he was joking. Was it possible that his campaign was an act? Maybe the whole thing is some kind of Joaquin Phoenix-esque performance art and he's not really a reactionary loony, but actually he's a progressive, lefty, liberal, artsy actor guy, who has created the character of a crazy monster to see how far it'll get him. It could be a piece of performance art brilliance so great as to eclipse even the fictional Oxford-based murders he used to solve with Kevin Whately. It's *that* good. Whether that one day turns out to be the truth, we shall have to wait and see. As for the mayoral election at hand, the advantage was mine. So much so that even Laurence himself conceded defeat:

Things were going well. So well that my Martian base was inundated with interview requests from the likes of the BBC, ITV and a young upstart by the name of Owen Jones, who I assumed was an enthusiastic schoolboy working on a GCSE politics project but who turned out to be a famous *Guardian* journalist. A fortnight before the election, Mr Jones personally opened a channel to me:

Owen: First Lord of the Universe, do you do interviews?

Binface: I've been known to dabble.

Owen: How do I message you?

Binface: You just did, old bean.

With contact established, Mr Jones and I then enjoyed a fruitful virtual chat about intergalactic politics, in which I was able to console him about the state of the Labour Party past and present:

Owen: The 2019 election was one of the worst days of my life.

Binface: Well, I'll tell you why. It was a two-horse race, and you backed a horse with no legs, which got shot in the car park before the race had even started.

Owen: I certainly felt like I'd been shot in the head in a car park. What about Keir Starmer, what do you make of him?

Binface: I think Keir is a well-meaning man. He hasn't, to my knowledge, turned an entire religious minority against the Labour Party. Yet. It's early days.

I was riding the crest of a wave. Bin-faced politics was more powerful than ever. By the time London went to the polls, the fine organs of the Fourth Estate were firmly on my side, with no fewer than three major newspapers featuring me on their front page. Even the *Spectator* was wooed by my fresh, sensible candidacy, with Nick Tyrone arguing in its esteemed pages, 'Why things have got to the point where I'm now considering voting for Count Binface as mayor' and 'Binface is weirdly one of the better candidates'. On the flipside, powerhouse chief political commentator John Rentoul published in the *Independent* a list of the top ten joke candidates of all time, in which I came top of the pops. Strange. It was almost as if John wasn't taking my manifesto seriously. Still, a win's a win.

And speaking of victory, that brings us back to the start of this chapter and the glorious 92,896 votes kindly given to me by London's Earthlings, with which I thrashed Piers Corbyn and UKIP, cemented my place as the ominverse's most powerful alien, and raised the important issue of competitively priced crois-sants. As if that wasn't enough, in 2022 a report in the *Evening Standard* revealed that my campaign was the most cost-effective of all twenty candidates. As their headline boomed, 'At just 40p per vote, Binface's mayoral backers didn't throw away their cash'. Quite right. You don't need an expensive advertising blitz when you've got the best policies, the best personality, and lasers.

Running to be London mayor was a huge step forward in my bid to conquer Earth. As a gentleman called Sam Heart wrote on Twitter, 'You may not have moved that hand-dryer yet, Count, but you have moved a city.' That's lovely to hear, but I want you to know that I'm not sitting on my laurels, or indeed my hardies. There's still lots to do, and that's what the rest of this book is about. I am here to show you a brighter future for every single citizen of the United Kingdom, except Jacob Rees-Mogg. It sounds fanciful, but together we can do it (well, I'll do it, you just have to vote for it).

Before we sort out your future, though, we need to have a proper look at how you got into this mess.

Part Two

The Rough Guide to Earth
(or How Did You Get into this Mess?)

Whenever I land on a new planet, I always think it's important to get to know the place. What's the gravity? Where's the free parking?*Are there any harmful microbes that could wipe out my species only a few weeks after arrival? Any alien who invades a new world without conducting elementary research like that should be thoroughly ashamed of themselves. I've heard that some Martians might have made just such a slip-up a century or so ago when they tried to invade a rich and bountiful territory named 'Woking'. Seriously, guys, that is just amateur hour. I was eager not to make such a cock-up myself when I reached Earth, so before arriving I decided to immerse myself in your history. What with your world being four billion years old, it didn't take long to spool through the highlights, as I'm sure you can imagine. I mean, honestly. You lot have been slumming it. No hover cars, no light speed, no nuclear fusion. Just *Candy Crush Saga*, *Emily in Paris* and Dubai. Still, there's always Ceefax, which until its

---

* I can recommend a field 2½ miles due south of Maidenhead town centre. It's perfect for a cloaked, galaxy-class starship. Unless you're a rambler who happens to unknowingly walk into the hull. I love it when that happens.

disgraceful abolition covered up a multitude of sins. And mark my words, one day it will again.

Learning about a world and its dominant civilisation never fails to be a useful tool for a space warrior, whether you're looking to conquer the planet and/or you want to clean up at pub quizzes (and if you ask me, you can't have the former without the latter). Of course sometimes there's no need to garner much knowledge about a place in order to achieve total domination. Take my neck of the galactic woods. One of the nearby planets to mine is Sigma II. It is populated by a humanoid species known as the Emojians, who can communicate only by means of basic hieroglyphs, depicting a series of rudimentary shapes such as faces, flags and long, shiny vegetables. They are of such stunted intelligence that there was no need to learn about their whole history before I subdued them. They were so busy sending each other inane messages, they didn't notice they'd been invaded. It's now forty Sigma years since I took control of them and they still haven't twigged. Fools like that are just there for the taking. ☺

Earthlings will no doubt be pleased to hear that on an interstellar scale, *Homo sapiens* is a relatively complex species (you're hovering just below average, like a kind of cosmic Everton). So it was no hardship for me to brush up on the history of the planet, and especially that of the territory which I had targeted for my primary invasion: the United Kingdom.

In the course of doing so, I made an important discovery, which is that the British have over a millennium's worth of experience in catastrophes, cataclysms and cock-ups. Once I'd become aware of this, the rise of Boris Johnson, and his self-inflicted fall, suddenly made a lot more sense. He's not an outlier, he's part of a long and inglorious trend. For humans, who are stuck inside the shitshow of current events, it can be hard to see the bigger picture, so I thought I'd take advantage of my objective, interstellar viewpoint to furnish you with a potted history of the UK that doesn't scrimp on the screw-ups (listen and learn, Schama).

It's an uncomfortable truth but your country's last thousand years have been a long, constantly diarrhoetic intestine of trouble. And you – reading this in the 2020s – are living at the sphincter's edge. After such an egregious era of error, it's never been more important to ask: how did it all get to this point? So now, for the first time ever on Earth, a politician is going to lay down the facts with a sober and impartial chronicle of crap.

Before we begin, I appreciate that my summary of Britain's past is not the first to be committed to print, but I guarantee that compared to any others mine will be the most accurate. If anyone should care to argue about that, let them answer this simple question: which one of us has had access to a time machine? Trust me, you can keep your epilators and your 'SodaStreams'. There is no finer piece of technology that a life form can hope to own than a time travel device, a fact I know all too keenly because frustratingly a few years ago I lost mine in the Asteroid Field of Fnor. Even more frustratingly, the one thing I'd need in order to locate it again is a time machine. It's very annoying.

Finally, a quick word about the focus of my summary. I know

I'm fairly new around here but it seems to me that the history syllabus in British schools has long been biased towards the English, neglecting the ups and downs of the Celtic warlords and the great Scottish monarchy. So in order to chime with the preferences of most readers (and hence voters), I have been careful to do the same.

OK then. If you're ready for a whistle-stop tour through Britain's Biggest Clangers* (or BBC for short), let's take a jump to the left,† and do a time warp.

AD 925

You don't know what happened then, do you? Nope, I thought not. And that's the first failing. I'll wager that the question of why AD 925 is important would stump pretty much anyone, whether you're a normal individual, an expert historian or David Starkey. The whole of humanity seems wrongly to have settled upon the idea that British history began with 1066 and all that. Don't worry, we'll get to that juicy date in a minute. But come on, humans, you can't just lazily write off everything that preceded that and brush it under the carpet as 'the Dark Ages'. The fault for this historic and indeed historical oversight lies with the Bayeux Tapestry, or the Bayeux Travesty as it should be known, for the way it has

---

* By Clangers I mean mistakes, as opposed to a species of high-pitched mouse-like vermin who used to infest a small hollow planet near mine, until they were exterminated by the Delonauts for health and safety reasons (understandable) and target practice reasons (less understandable).

† Assuming that you're not Jeremy Corbyn or one of his acolytes, in which case I appreciate this manoeuvre is physically impossible.

skewed humans' beliefs. Just because the Anglo-Saxons didn't bother to do what the Normans did, and weave their tale into a massive (i.e. poorly edited) comic strip, doesn't mean they don't have a cool tale to tell of their own. Schoolteachers would know this if they'd pulled their fingers out of their annus horribilis and spent years mastering the primitive Anglo-Saxon dialect instead of wasting free periods lusting after the new French assistant. But sadly humans are suckers for a pretty picture, so the Travesty has garnered way more attention than any of the exciting stuff that preceded it.

Now, before you start wondering if I've got some kind of weird grudge against the tapestry, and if perhaps its depiction of a fireball racing through the sky isn't a sighting of Halley's Comet as commonly believed, but is instead proof that my dad flew past Earth at this point in 1066 on a pleasure cruise with his mistress Vuzycla when he'd told all of us at home that he was on a work trip to Sigma III, let me assure you that nothing could be further from the truth. No siree. My qualms with it are purely professional. To understand the birth of your nation, I've personally scoured the original Anglo-Saxon sources – as any conscientious politician would – and so I don't need to rely on a giant, patterned souvenir scarf to tell me the story of Britain, and when it truly began. And that's what brings us to 925.

The reason it all kicked off then is that this was when some dude called King Athelstan united the two kingdoms of 'Mercia' and 'Wessex', using the old-fashioned pan-galactic diplomatic playbook of slaughtering all his opponents. He then drove the Vikings out of Northumbria, which is not to say that he gave them a lift to the nearest port, but rather that he slaughtered all his opponents. He really did have a penchant for slaughtering, that guy. Within two years he'd created the first sense of a united country on the British mainland. And to prove that this was the birth of England as we know it today, they promptly went and invaded Scotland. By his hatred of the Celts, King Athelstan proved that he was the real McCoy, a misleading phrase that confused him into nearly slaughtering himself. The year 925 may not be taught in human history classes, but it's the real start of British history, and it has at least been immortalised in song by that great twentieth-century historian, Dolly Parton.

As for everything that happened before Athelstan, we can write that off and brush it all under the carpet as the Dark Ages.

1066

There's no getting away from it. This is the most famous date that is drummed into British younglings when they are at school (apart from 2017, when I took on Mrs May). There are tens of thousands of Brits who can't remember their own partner's birthday but who will know when the Battle of Hastings took place. But this is strange, because while every other nation on Earth skews the history books towards its most glorious moments, there's no getting away from the fact that 1066 was a great big fat defeat for the home team. And not just that: to local rivals the French, of all people. I'd have thought you guys would have wanted to keep this humiliation very hush-hush indeed, but maybe it's just a sign of what makes it so British: it's a plucky defeat, a romantic failure, a 'Kevin Keegan" moment. And that's why I've included it in this compendium of cack.

In the decades leading up to the big battle, the crown of England had been passed around more than glandular fever in freshers' week. Not long after Athelstan the throne was inherited by the interestingly named Cnut, a fact that will be almost exactly repeated when Prince Charles succeeds his mother. Cnut remains one of England's first famous kings and, according to an unlikely legend in which he claimed he could 'hold back the tide', he was one of the wettest too. He was also the galaxy's second most afflicted ruler by the curse of the typo, after the current tyrant of Theta V, Marshall FuthaMukka. Both these poor souls have my sympathies, given the potential issues with the English spelling of my own name (the 'o' is very important).

---

* Human football personality who in 1996, as manager of Newcastle United FC, turned the act of snatching defeat from the jaws of victory into an art form. Unbeknownst to Mr Keegan, his fame has spread further than he knows. Transmissions of Premier League football have travelled into space and footage of the 1995–6 season was intercepted by the Oorxonians, a nomadic tribe whose mothership happened to be passing by Earth in 1996. They promptly got hooked on the title race, but owing to a backlog of home-grown drama box sets which they hadn't yet got round to watching, the Oorxonians' central computer had a data storage issue which meant that it stopped recording signals before the final weeks of the season. Blithely assuming that Newcastle couldn't throw away a twelve-point lead to Manchester United and that they must have won the title, the Oorxonians worshipped Mr Keegan as a god and dedicated to him their most sacred prayer, 'Myt Plooska Runxit Nmyaabonx', which translates as 'I would love it if we beat them'. Oorxonian Chief Psooki even changed his name to Keegan as a good luck gesture, just before they embarked on an interstellar war with their great rivals the Nimbari. Appropriately enough, in true Keegan style the Oorxonians came a very close second in the war. Which is to say that they all got massacred.

Cnut passed on the crown – and the likelihood of being bullied at school – to his son, whom he named Harthacnut. Human schoolbooks have it that poor Harthacnut was succeeded by the more soberly named Edward the Confessor, but even this is merely a half-truth. For Edward did in fact rule jointly with his twin brother John. Together John and Edward (known collectively as Jedewarde) were more interested in the arts than medieval statecraft, and they formed an ill-starred partnership that would serenade the querulous court with tone-deaf duets, until one day the barons demanded that Edward choose between his brother and the crown; in an outrageous act of gross heartlessness, Edward chose his brother, provoking the barons to murder John in his sleep. This explains the king's famous nickname: between causing his twin's death and doing tortuous cover versions of folk minstrel standards, Edward had plenty to confess.

Edward finally died on 5 January 1066, and with the demise of Jedewarde there opened up a power vacuum in England. This had the French licking their lips, and they duly organised an invasion led by William, the Duke of Normandy. William, who was also known as William the Bastard, lived in a settlement established by Charles the Simple, who was the son of Louis the Stammerer and who had initially been denied the throne of West Francia by his cousin, Charles the Fat.* And the inhabitants of England lost to this lot. I'll just leave that here.

---

* To think that some human journalists have had the cheek to suggest that *my* name sounds stupid. If you ask me, people in glass houses shouldn't throw stones. Or, not to put too fine a point on it, humans on fragile planets shouldn't insult a space warrior in possession of a laser-armed battle fleet.

William's forces landed in Sussex on 28 September 1066, in the millennium's first recorded example of migrants making an unchecked Channel crossing. (I don't understand why twenty-first-century Conservatives are so fearful about how migrant crossings might damage the status quo, when it is in fact directly responsible for the line of succession. It's almost as if people like Nigel Farage and Priti Patel haven't read enough books.) The famed battle between William's Normans and King Harold's Saxon defenders took place on 14 October in a fierce clash of arms, which left behind a terrible mess that to this day is known as Hastings. Afterwards, the victorious Duke became King of England and gained a new moniker: William the Conqueror. Which is a bit over the top if you ask me, after just one flash in the pan. It's akin to the singer of 'The One and Only' being referred to as Chesney Hawkes the Conqueror. Still, although he was a bit full of himself – like all royal Williams – he was a successful king and from 1066 onwards Norman influence spread from the south coast across the country, a phenomenon that happened again in the late 1990s with Fatboy Slim. William also commissioned the first comprehensive national census, known as the Domesday Book. This is not to be confused with the *Doomsday* Book, which is a fair review of any novel written by Nadine Dorries.

1215

This was the year that saw the sealing of Magna Carta (or 'Great Charter'), one of the most important and problematic documents on planet Earth and, in its biggest failing, one of the least read.

Billions of humans have never heard of the damn thing, let alone taken a shufti at it, and yet it is held up by your species as being the cornerstone of modern democracy. Well, being a conscientious space warrior I always like to do my research, so one quiet evening over a lovely drop of WD40 I gave it a peruse to see what all the fuss is about, and I urge you to do the same (the reading, not the drinking of industrial lubricants. I'm not Donald Trump).

The gist of Magna Carta is pretty simple: it's a peaceful show of strength by a nation's subjects against their ruler, King John, who's deemed by common consent to be the worst king in England's history.* The 4,478-word agreement was a step forwards on your planet's long journey towards universal human freedom, securing the right to a fair trial for everyone who counted (i.e. not women or slaves), and making a smattering of Latin seem important and clever. Fair enough. But if you ask me, plenty more of the document is completely insane.

The bit that most caused my optical organs to pop out of my visor is this: 'No town or person shall be forced to build bridges over rivers except those with an ancient obligation to do so.'

In my humble opinion, if you need to put into writing the idea of ending compulsory bridge-building for all citizens, you're doing politics wrong. To be generous to the thirteenth-century Englanders who wrote it, there is another possible explanation for this madness. It could be a classic example of medieval society taking things too literally, in this case the saying that 'it's better

---

* Although it's definitely worth putting a fiver on Charles III finding a way to eclipse him.

to build bridges than walls'. Whatever the reason, it's a pan-galactic truth that you can tell a lot about a civilisation from their policy towards bridges: as we shall see on page 167, it's a key way that I have been able to differentiate my manifesto from that of Boris Johnson. As for the good people of AD 1215, Magna Carta suggests in stark terms that they might have been a bit simple.

This brings me neatly to my next point, which is that Magna Carta is in many ways the perfect precursor of Boris Johnson's 2019 Brexit Agreement: it's a shame that it was needed, much of its text is a load of old guff, and most notably, the person in charge of the country who signed it almost immediately went back on the deal. As with King John, so with King Boris. When will humans learn that a liar's signature is worth less than a CD copy of *Rudebox* by Robbie Williams? Over in my galactic quadrant we see this kind of deceitful skulduggery all the time. Take Idilia Frax, for instance, the former First Minister of Sigma X. She agreed to a 'Bill of Universal Rights', which was set to improve the quality of life for more than twenty billion citizens, and which led to her winning a landslide in the subsequent general election. It sounded great. But when Idilia got round to publishing the Bill after the vote, she cunningly listed it in bookstores in the fiction section, meaning she didn't have to go through with a single word of it. By anyone's estimation, that was a sneaky move. But there was a silver lining: her Bill of Rights never made it to number one in the book charts. Even on Sigma X it was beaten into second place by the indomitable Richard Osman.

1346

Speaking of highly transmissible phenomena, next up in our anthology of arse-ups we come to the Black Death. It swept across Europe, killing roughly half of the entire human population of Eurasia. This makes 1346 a date that will live in infamy, along with 1941 for the attack on Pearl Harbor, and 2001 for the release of Michael Bay's *Pearl Harbor*. The exact origin of Britain's first recorded pandemic is unknown, but suspicion tends to fall upon the ships that were arriving at Dover and Southampton from mainland Europe, bringing home monks who were returning from the Italian ski season. Public anger at the government's lack of support for those afflicted with the virus spawned the Black Deaths Matter movement and also originated the phenomenon of 'taking the knee', which at that point people carried out not as an honourable gesture of solidarity but as an involuntary consequence of coughing up their lungs and collapsing in the mud.

1483–5

This two-year period saw the short, ill-starred reign of Richard III, who to this day stands accused of conniving to have his two young nephews murdered in the Tower of London: your planet's original 'Dick move'. After defeat to Henry Tudor at the Battle of Bosworth Field, Richard's naked and lifeless body was dragged through the streets of Leicester city centre, a fate that you can see being re-enacted there by revellers most Saturday nights. Richard

III is arguably the most controversial leader in British history.* Was he a hideous, child-murdering hunchback or a good king whose reputation has been trashed in the centuries since? The truth is neither. His real place in history is as a portent for the history of the Labour Party. In having to deal with a winter of discontent he foreshadowed the woes of the James Callaghan government of 1978; in being demonised as an evil and corrupt prick before having his reputation gradually rise in the public's estimation, Richard's career is an exact mirror image of Tony Blair's.

1509

This year saw the accession of Henry VIII. Possibly England's most famous monarch, as well as its most rotund, Henry set the standard for bending the rules to suit his every whim, making him the original wide boy in more ways than one. He was also in some senses a very modern man, such as in his liberal attitude to dating and gastronomy, and I can't help thinking he would have thrived as a ruler on the moons of Grumio, where it is customary that when you are done with your spouse, you eat him or her. I don't have any evidence that Henry VIII did that, but at the same time I also don't have any proof that he didn't. Seeing as cannibalism is supposed to drive you mad, it would explain a lot.

Henry began life as merely the second in line to the throne, after his older brother Arthur. Henry, or Harry as he was known to his mates, was the heir presumptive's younger, more annoying

---

* Give or take Boris.

and more ginger sibling, known around court for having a controversial love life and a craving for the limelight. Notoriety dogged him through youth, especially when he was caught attending a jig dressed up as a member of the Spanish Inquisition. If it weren't for Arthur's untimely demise, Henry's life would have been nothing but a historical footnote, most notable for setting up 'Ye Olde Invictus Jousting Tournamente' for retired knights. As it was, he inherited the English throne and by the time he died in 1547 he had become the archetype for a Western leader in possession of absolute power: a corpulent, orange mess of a man, with a penchant for wanting to lock people up. If he was alive now he'd no doubt own a string of golf courses and be the guest judge on a major TV reality show.

1553

Don't let human historians tell you that the industrial revolution began in 1760. That's just another example of Earthlings airbrushing their own history. The true starting date is 1553, when Queen Mary I put the proverbial rocket boosters under the British economy with the discovery of an exciting new fuel: Protestants. For a brief five-year period, you couldn't move for the sight of public squares being heated by heretics, until Bloody Mary died and was succeeded by her sister Elizabeth I, who was herself a Protestant and not a fan of self-immolation. In 1558, Good Queen Bess took immediate action to clean up this dirty fuel by creating a Catholic converter, which became mandatory for all citizens – on pain of death.

Incidentally, whether you take the start date of industrialisation to be 1553 or 1760, either way it means that from the emergence of *Homo sapiens*, it took your species 300,000 years to reach this important milestone. That makes you guys officially the slowest 'advanced' life form to get there, beating the Boneheaded Knuckle-Draggers of Eltar into last place. If you're interested, it took the Knuckle-Draggers 209,456 Earth years to begin industrialising. They would have got there quicker but for the fact they made the mistake of inventing Wordle first.

1605

Remember, remember, the fifth of November, the gunpowder, treason and plot.
I see of no reason why the gunpowder treason should ever be forgot.

Quite right. Why wouldn't you want to remember the biggest loser in British history? Guy Fawkes is literally the guy who tried to blow up the Houses of Parliament but was caught in the act, hiding in an undercroft of the palace surrounded by barrel upon barrel of explosives. He initially protested his innocence, in the least convincing denial ever seen until 'It Wasn't Me' by Shaggy and 'There was no party' by Boris Johnson. Fawkes is as famous for his punishment as for his crime: he was sentenced for attempted sedition to being hung, drawn and quartered. But of course there was a fourth element to his comeuppance: having a whole day in the calendar named after him, specifically to rub his nose in it for being such an unmitigated failure. For centuries, humans have ritually spent the night of 5 November setting fire to things and creating explosions in the sky, just to show how easy it is. Into the twenty-first century, the infamy of Fawkes has grown even further, with the 'Anonymous' group of hackers starting a trend in which anti-establishment protestors conceal their identity by wearing masks with his face on them. This would annoy Guy Fawkes no end, because remaining anonymous was something he singularly failed to do.

I'm not one for dumbing down history – I'm quite happy leaving that to Neil Oliver – but if I have one suggestion about how to commemorate the events of 1605, it's with the famous rhyme, which is clearly in need of an update. I'm a charitable kind of space warrior, so for you, dear reader, I offer this alternative:

Remember, remember, the bell-ended member, who cocked up his terrorist plot.

Firework season's the excellent reason why pets everywhere love him not.

There have of course been subsequent failed attempts to destroy Parliament, such as in 1940 by the Luftwaffe and in 2019 by Dominic Cummings, an old friend of these pages, who swapped high explosives for a new type of incendiary device: a failed revamp of civil service office space, followed by a stream of bitter and bitchy think-piece blog-rants (or so I've heard – there's no way I'm subscribing to that weirdo and misfit's Substack newsletter).

1665

This year saw the arrival in Britain of the Plague, aka *Black Death II: Sick In the City*. It was the second outbreak of the same illness to ravage the planet in 326 years,* and arguably more famous than the first. In essence this sequel was a pale retread of events back in 1346, owing to a lack of imagination on the part of the virus. But for the humans who had to live through it, the seventeenth-century pandemic was more than horrible enough to endure. Citizens had no choice but to live in fear, waiting with bated (and infectious) breath for the next daily parchment from Sir Christoph de Whittye, the government's chief apothecary, while signs all over the country implored peasants to observe the three cardinal rules: 'Handseth. Faceth. Spaceth.' Seeing as the majority of the population was illiterate, and running water was quite literally a pipe dream, this signage policy was a costly error, and it led to the death sentence for its administrator, Lord Matthew de Handcocke.

Eventually more stringent measures were required to solve the crisis and King Charles II took the unprecedented step of ordering England's first ever national lockdown, which forced a whole season of executions to take place behind closed doors (although an exception was made for Handcocke). Theatre was also affected, with a raft of closures that saw the cancellation of a huge planned season of Shakespeare comedies. In a time of suffering and without vaccines, this news did at least provide some relief.

Also on the bright side, the plague experience inspired many of those who survived to discover new ways to flourish and display

* If the boys and girls at the Wuhan lab are reading this, that's not a record Earth should really be aiming at breaking. So for the planet's sake, please keep your bio-suits zipped up at all times.

their resourcefulness, including the creation of the world's first sourdough starter. This new bread was so health-giving that some people even wondered if it could bestow the gift of immortality. Such talk was a silly exaggeration, claimed the inventor of sourdough, a woman by the name of Mary Berry, who in 1665 was a sprightly fifty-eight years old. Even so, thanks to Mary, home baking became a craze which spread across the country faster than the virus, and it even indirectly helped to end London's plague in the following year...

1666

Sunday 2 September 1666 was a key cock-up in the history of the Earth capital, seeing as it did the start of the Great Fire of London. Many humans know that the conflagration began in a bakery on Pudding Lane, but the identity of the fire-starter* has always been more of a mystery. I can't pinpoint a perpetrator for you, but I can reveal that a severely singed sausage roll was discovered at the scene, and that for weeks afterwards fingers were pointed at a local grocer called Greg. In order to avoid suspicion, he adopted a brilliant disguise of adding an extra 'g' at the end of his name, and from that point on his family wealth went from strength to strength.

1707

The Act of Union occurred this year, bringing together the unstoppable English force of overbearing arrogance and the immovable

---

* The twisted fire-starter.

Scottish object of having a chip on your shoulder into the world's longest and unhappiest geopolitical marriage. And they all lived miserably ever after, until _____. (I'll let you fill in the gap when the big split finally comes.)

1837

Queen Victoria's reign began this year, and is often looked back upon fondly as one of Britain's most glorious periods. But it's also synonymous with 'Empire', which these days is a dirty word. And not just on your planet. On the opposite spiral arm of your Milky Way galaxy there lives a species called the Hulannians, who used to crave interstellar domination. For an epoch or two they really were the Billy Big Balls of their solar system, and they ruled the gamma waves. But then the silly sausages went and overreached themselves and bankrupted their economy, leaving them to rue their past ambition and forcing them to make grubby arms deals with some questionably-run, fuel-producing planets to make ends meet. In a bid to save face, the Hulannians decided to stop using the word Empire and to start calling their depleted chain of colonies a 'Commonwealth' of planets instead, but they weren't fooling anyone. These days the only remaining vestige of their civilisation's once remarkable power is an absurd annual concert which they stage every year in their capital city, where citizens sing songs like 'Rule Hulannia' and bob up and down in a ritual motion, looking like galaxy-leading prats. Bless 'em.

As for Earth, one potent remaining symbol of the Victorian imperial mindset is the British Museum, a treasure trove of items ~~stolen~~ lovingly curated from ~~the rightful owners~~ around your planet. The most controversial of its priceless artefacts are sculptures from the Parthenon, also known as the 'Elgin Marbles' after Lord Elgin, who ~~ransacked~~ recovered them from Athens. For decades the Greek government has demanded that the United Kingdom return these priceless assets but the Brits have stood firm. Well, I agree with Greece, and I hereby pledge in this book that ~~if~~ when I take power on planet Earth I will as a matter of urgency hand back the missing blocks of the frieze.

'Why?' A reader may ask.

'Because they're nicked,' I shall reply.

'But if you give the marbles back, other countries will start wanting their stuff back too,' they will moan.

'So what?' I will shrug.

'Because then the British Museum will end up empty,' they will cry.

'You mean it will open up a giant cultural void?' I will ask.

'Exactly,' they will confirm.

'I can't think of a more perfect memorial to Brexit Britain,' I shall declare. 'Trust me, if that was to happen, visitor numbers to the museum would go up.' And I will saunter away from my defeated interlocutor with a satisfied flourish of my cloak.

1903–13

The 1900s saw the emergence of the suffragettes, who are without doubt some of the most heroic humans in this strange country's history. So why include these brave female activists in a list of the UK's biggest failures? Because it seems weird to me that a nation that supposedly bases its whole political system on what the majority wants could routinely treat the majority (i.e. women) far worse than the minority (men). It's almost as if human men have deliberately sewn up society for themselves. After sucking up generation upon generation of unfair suppression, the suffragettes demanded that it was high time for women to be allowed to vote. Ideally they were after a bit more than that – full equality would have been nice – but for starters they at least wanted to have a say over which men told them what to do. And that pretty much brings us up to date on where Britain has got with this issue. Yes, I appreciate that in the last 100 Earth years, women have finally been allowed to vote in elections, stand for election and even occasionally become Prime Minister. But even I can see that the cards are still stacked. If you ask me, women will only have achieved a semblance of equality when at least half the world leaders are women, half of MPs are women, and Jeremy Clarkson has been vaporised on live television. Ladies, I am here to tell you I want all of those things, and you'll be pleased to hear that I'm pursuing the latter with particular vigour.

1914

This year saw the start of the conflict which humans named the Great War: so great was it, in fact, that they decided to have a second one a couple of decades later. It is quite possibly the most horrific clash of arms ever fought on Earth's soil, and in every way a perversion of normal life. For proof, just look at the

1914 Christmas truce, when the two sides stopped fighting on 25 December – the polar opposite of how millions of families spend that day now.

As for the British army during the period 1914–18, never in the field of human conflict were so many soldiers sacrificed for so little gain by so few brain cells. The quality of Britain's generals left a lot to be desired, and the most infamous of the lot was Field Marshal Sir Douglas Haig, who managed to command the British army despite labouring under the misapprehension that machine-gun fire is repelled by human skin. Few military officers on Earth have such a chequered reputation as Haig, but he could take some solace from the fact that in the wider cosmos he is in plentiful company.

To my knowledge, the omniverse's all-time most notorious strategist is Othkonok, admiral of the Craveen, whose insatiable appetite for conquest led him to make an audacious bid to control the incredibly powerful Pantares. Othkonok had already conquered most of his solar system, but even the most hawkish voices among the Craveen wondered if this time their leader might have bitten off more than he could chew, seeing as Pantares was their sun, a red giant roughly fifty times hotter than Earth's local star. But Othkonok would brook no argument and he dismissed any dissenting generals from service, and indeed the surface, blasting their bodies into space for displaying insubordination. Then he loaded a battle cruiser full of 500,000 crack troops and, while he watched from a distance, ordered the ship to fly straight at Pantares, in case the star might surrender to him. The expedition went just about as well as you'd expect, with the troops all frying to death and the cruiser melting into goo before they were a million miles from the surface. On his homecoming from the catastrophe back on Craveen, Othkonok was treated in a way the British would recognise all too well: he was made a high-ranking lord and given three million space credits to enjoy a groovy retirement.

The 1920s

This was a remarkable decade for humanity, which began with a renewed sense of hope after years of armed conflict, and ended with politicians proving they were equally capable of causing total chaos in peacetime as well as war. In the UK, 1924 saw the arrival of the first Labour government in Britain: whether that fact on its own counts as a historic success or failure will depend on your point of view. But there are certainly a few details here that are objectively worthy of mention in our catalogue of crud. It was Ramsay MacDonald who led the party to power by cobbling together a brief minority administration, and legions of Labour voters reacted to his victory in typical style, decrying him for shamelessly selling out and going so far as to kick him out of the party. Even more impressively, in 1929 Ramsay worked his way back and became PM on a second occasion, this time winning a majority for Labour, which for many on the left of the party was even more unforgivable.

The 1940s

I include this decade in our conglomeration of codswallop not to shine a light on the Second World War, but on the baby boom that followed it. I must confess that, not being from Earth, when I first heard the phrase 'baby boom' I was horrified. 'That's what you guys do in *peacetime*?' I wondered. Not even Vortigua the Immortal Gravity Beast is that cruel. But then I discovered that the phrase instead refers to the offspring from a national sexual extravaganza that was ignited by the end-of-war festivities. It seems there's nothing more arousing for British consenting adults than a celebration involving bunting, cakes and cream teas. This is presumably the real explanation for the mysterious success of the *Great British Bake Off*: It's a highly potent aphrodisiac, causing soggy bottoms throughout the land.

Back to the baby boomers: they are to a large extent responsible for the world as you know it today. Some would say they've taken the lessons learned from the Second World War and used them to help ensure that such a devastating conflict never happens again. Others might say that they've rigged the jobs market, housing market, stock market, pensions system, legal system and indeed the entire political system to their advantage, kicking the ladder away from future generations and crushing social mobility for the next century. The truth is of course both. Being born just after the war, the boomers couldn't remember first-hand the way in which one powerful force could overrun Western Europe, which makes it all the more astonishing that they have managed to re-enact it so perfectly.

The 1960s

The 'Swinging Sixties' was a halcyon, much-idolised moment in the UK's history, when its cultural scene blazed a trail across the world. I don't want to rain on your parade or anything, but the truth is that every planet experiences a 'swinging' decade. Our one on Sigma IX was a blast, man. It was so out there that we all stopped work, blasted off from the surface and spent it partying on our moons. I don't remember much of it, but it was certainly a hip and happening time, when the lids were getting longer and the liners were getting shorter. Swing bins came in, and the iconic model Binny was on the cover of pretty much every e-mag and robo-billboard. Happy days.

As for Britain in the Sixties, leading the way were popular beat combo the Beatles, who became an immediate smash hit with their single 'Love Me Do', monetising the art of garbled syntax nearly two decades before George Lucas and Yoda repeated the same trick. Of course, not even the Beatles' reputation has emerged unscathed by the passage of time. With one hand Paul McCartney giveth 'Hey Jude', and with the other he writeth the frog song.

A key year in this period was 1966, which has become a byword for England winning the World Cup. As a result it's up there with the other famous '66, 900 years earlier, among the most well-known dates in the country's history. And at least they won this one. (Or did they? I won't kick that hornet's nest. Although if I did kick it, I'd make sure it went over the line.)

Rounding off the decade, on 20 July 1969 humans landed

on the moon. This is often hailed as the single most impressive achievement in human history. On the flipside, for us aliens it's the equivalent of popping to the local corner shop for some toilet roll and a Double Decker. But well done everyone. In the years of the Apollo missions twelve men visited the lunar surface, and they used their time there to play novelty golf, joyride in buggies and drink wine, all while wearing matching outfits. So it was less a science expedition and more a stag do. You can see why the rest of the omniverse is glad that you guys haven't got the ability to travel any further: the last thing planet Ulavis needs is a herd of tanked-up blokes in Smurf suits pissing into its volcanoes. It's an intergalactic heritage site, not Prague.

The 1990s

This belongs in our cavalcade of cobblers because of 'Cool Britannia', a strange phenomenon in which the decade was defined by a lazy rehash of cultural trends from the 1960s, such as social liberation, footballing optimism and mop-topped guitar bands. Looking back at it now, was this really a vision of Britannia that was *cool*, or was it one that had been left out of the fridge for too long and near a radiator before being reheated in a microwave and washed down with a gallon of Hooch? Some readers will know the answer to this. I wasn't there at the time, but I can hazard a guess.

As I did my research on this period, I was briefly angered by the thought that humans had developed a massive craze for a rival space warrior, but then I discovered that it was bucket *hats* that you guys had got into, and that's fine. Choosing to wear silly headgear like that just makes people look ridiculous, if you ask me, but, hey, it's your planet. (For now).

In 1992 the Queen suffered her 'annus horribilis', and just a year later in 1993 planet Earth experienced an 'annus horribilissimus', when the eponymous debut single by an artist called Mr Blobby secured the coveted Christmas number one slot, at a stroke making the slot substantially less coveted. This portly pink popster's unlikely success was a sign of the decaying times and it led to a number of spin-offs including some for his sidekick character: a tiny, bizarre, hirsute bipedal creature with a penchant for house parties by the name of Edmonds, who was very much a hairy Robin to Blobby's Batman. Elsewhere in the cosmos, this year saw an astonishing scientific breakthrough as my Recyclon engineers on Sigma IX created the omniverse's first working Ironoscope – a device which can measure Irony Waves through space. (Irony can behave as either a particle or a wave. It's complicated so just trust me on this one.) The machine was able to measure signals for precisely nine and a quarter Earth hours, until D:Ream released their song 'Things Can Only Get Better', whereupon it promptly exploded.

2012

At last we move into the twenty-first century, and the occasion of the London Olympic and Paralympic Games. For one brief moment it seemed like everything was rosy in the British garden and that perhaps you might not need help from a galactic overlord like me: everyone already seemed to be united under the rule of a benevolent, ubiquitous life form named 'Clare Balding'.

And then, of course, everything went wrong. It was almost as if, on the night of Danny Boyle's spectacular opening ceremony, you guys opened up a wormhole to a parallel universe, where hundreds of Mary Poppinses* rained down from the sky, the queen pretended to skydive with Daniel Craig, and the entire planet cheered the sight of David Beckham on a speedboat. Meanwhile, down on ground level an army of volunteers dressed up as doctors and nurses to celebrate the NHS and jived around hospital beds, goading Mother Nature to come up with a new virus to wipe the smiles off their faces. Little did they know that only eight years later, their costumed cavorting would be enough to qualify them for frontline care duties.

And the thing is, I must inform you, on that totemic night in the Olympic stadium the human race really did open up a wormhole into a parallel universe. (It hasn't escaped my notice that supervillain Sir Tim Berners Lee was at the ceremony, typing away on a computer before hitting the return key with a satisfying thunk. Did he unleash a rupture in the space-time continuum? He hasn't denied it. 'Nuff said.) But the point is that from this moment onwards, the timeline of Earth was left vulnerable to skewing off into an entirely new and dangerous direction. All it needed was one seismic event to set off a chain reaction that would cause your planet to spiral out of control. And it happened two years later.

---

* I think that's the plural. Apologies to Susie Dent if I'm wrong.

2014

Everything built up to this. Winning the Second World War. The industrial revolution. The Reformation. King Athelstan. The dinosaurs. The primordial soup. All four billion years of Britain's history, the whole kit and caboodle,* has been defined by a single moment that occurred on 21 May 2014, just after 6.30 a.m. It's an occasion that not only crowns this chronological corpus of cretinism, but which has set humanity on the dark path you are all currently following. For this was the instant when, at New Covent Garden Market, during a short break from choosing a bunch of flowers for his wonderful wife, Labour Party leader Ed Miliband attempted to eat a bacon sandwich.

Out of curiosity and awe for how Mr Miliband's decision has impacted your planet in the years since, I have taken the trouble to visit this crucial landmark. The scene of the crime. There I have watched as humans walk past, hither and thither, seemingly oblivious to the location's significance. Such ignorance is highly confusing to me. It's like they're in denial. The exact spot, where Ed failed to wrap his mouth around a medium-sized meat-filled snack, is more important than Stonehenge, the Giant's Causeway or even the Woking branch of Pizza Express. It needs to be marked with a commemorative plaque. A big, red plaque.

I'm assuming that children are taught all about this story in schools as a matter of course, but for the sake of completeness I

---

* My favourite English word.

shall recount the full, fateful fable. Mr Miliband was the younger brother of a man called David, who was a high-flying tyro in the governments of Mr Blair and Mr Brown. In 2010, after defeat at the general election, David had been tipped to become the next Labour leader and steer the party back to power. He seemed to have only two weaknesses: one, he liked Tony Blair, which is an obvious drawback; and two, he was once photographed holding a banana and looking like a bit of a prat. Little did David know then that the insurmountable obstacle between him and his dream would be neither of these things but something much closer to home: his younger brother.

Really, the silly fool should have seen it coming. Little Ed had been hunting and haunting Big David for the preceding twenty Earth years, choosing to pursue the very same degree course at exactly the same college at precisely the same university, before choosing to follow an identical career path at the same employer. If you have a smaller sibling and they tried it on like that, slavishly copying your every move, you might tell them to piss off and get a life.* Vortigua the Immortal Gravity Beast also used to have a younger sister, for instance, and she ate her. But where others would have raged, David showed mercy and stomached his brother's pitiful lack of imagination. This clemency proved to be a mistake, and decades later David's weakness came back to bite him on the centrist arse. Ed realised that his brother's dream was in fact his own ambition too, and

---

* There are other ways that having a controversial younger brother can be a hard thing to shake off. Just ask Prince Charles.

that rather than supporting his brother and waiting his turn for the Labour throne, he could strike now, seduce the trade unions and grab glory for himself. In the ensuing contest, Ed fractionally defeated David by 50.7 per cent to 49.3 per cent, detonating a lifetime of brotherly love for the chance to be viciously attacked by the right-wing press on a weekly basis for the next five years. Each to their own.

But Ed's aggressive move left him prey to the gods of poetic justice, and four years later karma duly delivered, in delicious snack form. The idea that eating a bacon sandwich could destroy a career and irrevocably change the course of human history is an outlandish one, but it's slightly less outrageous than the pig's ear he made out of trying to eat it. There's no getting around the fact that, for all his undoubted intellect, the man was a bit of a spanner, and that his attempt at sandwich consumption was a failure of galactic proportions.

Words cannot do justice to the extraordinary range of pained expressions which Mr Miliband's face contorted itself into that morning, as it strived to accomplish this most basic of motor skills. Well, no words in English can, at any rate. We Recyclons do have a noun to describe this very happenstance: 'Lembitopikoia'. It just so happened that the incident was caught on camera, to Ed's deep frustration, and to brother David's immense satisfaction. And thus began a mammoth chain reaction from which Earth is reeling to this very day.

The Conservative Party ruthlessly attacked Ed for his culinary handicap, which was a bit rich seeing as their leader – David Cameron – had a highly questionable relationship with pigs of his own,* but the Tories successfully convinced the British public that crippling austerity with them was better than 'chaos' with Ed, and at the 2015 election they secured an unexpected majority in the House of Commons. Esteemed human historians, such as W. I. Kipedia, assert that it is 'unclear what effect, if any, the photograph of Mr Miliband had on the eventual result' of the election. With my greater intellect and insight, I can fill in the blank and let you know precisely how impactful the photo was: 100 per cent.

But far more important than that is what happened next: a classic example of the Butterfly Effect, except a butterfly made out of cured pork and with a clumsy bite taken out of it. Ed Miliband's failings kept the Tories in Downing Street, which led David Cameron to become excessively cocky, which seduced him into gambling Britain's future on an EU referendum, which provoked Boris Johnson to fight against him to position himself as a future Conservative leader, which enabled a cabal of crazies including Nigel Farage and Dominic Cummings to run amok, which wrong-footed mainstream politicians, which allowed barefaced lies about the European Union to drown out the facts, which encouraged Russia to flood the internet with fake news, which helped to swing the referendum in favour of 'Vote Leave', which tore Britain out of the world's largest trading bloc, which emboldened populist politicians the world over to see that democracies were more vulnerable than ever, which meant that a new normal

---

* An unofficial biography of Mr Cameron claimed that once, while a student of Politics, Philosophy and Economics at Oxford University, he placed his penis inside the mouth of a dead pig. It's not clear which part of the course required him to do so, but my money's on Politics.

now prevailed, which emboldened Donald Trump's presidential campaign, which journalists found a macabre joy in covering, which helped to legitimise his candidacy, which set back the course of international relations several decades.

And that's just for starters. We don't have the space here to detail the full, near-infinite number of catastrophes that have unfolded directly as a result of Ed Miliband wrapping his lips around a bacon sarnie, but suffice to say that wars, economic hardship and the movie version of *Cats* are all his fault, as is everything bad that has happened since, except the coronavirus pandemic, which we can't fairly lay at Ed's door. Assuming that on that ill-starred morning it was just a bacon sandwich he was eating. It's hard to see from the photo but there might be a bat wing poking out of it. I can't be sure, but frankly I wouldn't be surprised.

While the mis-eating incident was Ed's fault and nobody else's, he's not solely responsible for causing the ripple effect that has set planet Earth on the path to destruction. Who is the most culpable? The photographer for immortalising the repulsive image? The newspaper editors for splashing the horror of it all over their front pages? The pig for being so damn tasty in the first place? The truth, of course, is all of them.

When it comes to destroying your planet, ultimately you're all in it together. It's just that Ed Miliband is the ringleader and he deserves a million years in prison. (I'm a merciful overlord so I shall let him keep recording his cosy podcast from his cell, which should keep him happy enough. I also won't tell him that none of the episodes are being published – what he doesn't know can't hurt him.)

And what of his erstwhile opponent during those dangerous days of the 2010s, Mr David Cameron? I'm sure you're wondering what his fate should be. The Phantom Zone. Obvs.

The Present Day

So there we are. That's the real history of Britain in an unvarnished and unflinching nutshell, and the real explanation for how Boris Johnson could possibly become the Prime Minister of an industrialised nation with a nuclear arsenal. As the UK moves into the post-Boris era, it couldn't be clearer that Count Binface is the perfect choice to be your new leader, for many reasons, not least because he doesn't like bacon, and he only rarely refers to himself in the third person.

Change is needed on Earth. But change to what? It's time to dig a little deeper.

Part Three

Choices, Choices

Whatever world you live in, if you're unfortunate enough to have to share it with other members of the dominant species, sooner or later you're going to need to have a political system. It's a drag but you can't get away from it. Like James Corden. When it comes to picking a system there's plenty of choice out there in the omniverse, and the key to achieving planetary harmony is simply to find the right option for the right species. This is something which *Homo sapiens* has proved to be spectacularly bad at doing. Humans have tried a fair few alternatives over the years and, as if you need me to tell you, they've all pretty much failed. The only question is deciding which one will fail the least catastrophically. Luckily, now all of that can change, thanks to me. What your planet has been lacking is a full, comprehensive guide to the different types of government that are available in space, together with their pros and cons. And that's where I come in. As a public service to you poor, struggling Earthlings, I am only too happy to present you with the full *à la carte* menu of ways that you can run the show. Almost all of them are risky, but you've got to pick one.

The Count Binface High-Stakes House
Presents
An À La Carte Menu of Political Systems

Primi
i.e. Who Gets the Keys to the Car?

Aristocracy

Favoured by human philosophers like Plato, aristocracy is supposed to mean 'rule by the best'. This is akin to the system that we currently have on Sigma IX, because I'm in charge. But on Earth, aristocracy ends up turning into a whole different can of flesh worms. Practically speaking, for humans it tends to deteriorate into rule by vested interests, with power being handed down through generations among a self-serving, self-proclaimed 'elite'. In essence, it promotes the idea of a world governed by Jacob Rees-Mogg. To be avoided.

Aristocatcracy

Rule by adorable, jazz-playing mammals of the genus *Felis*. This system is as yet untried on any planet, to my knowledge. It is marginally preferable to Earth's version of aristocracy, but I'd also steer clear of this one.

Absolute monarchy

Rule by a king or queen, whose qualification for the role consists of their DNA. Ultimately every carbon-based life form depends upon its DNA, but not in an idiotic way like this. Some kings and queens have been known to proclaim that they were appointed to the role by divine right, but without exception they were talking out of their rectum. Not just in the UK but across space, the traditional job of an absolute monarch is to fight battles, persecute minorities, sire an heir, sit for the odd portrait, get fat, grow old, go mad and die. Rarely are they successful in every category, but you get the odd one who achieves a full house (see Henry VIII in Earth's history, and George VII in Earth's future). Over the course of time, an absolute monarchy tends to atrophy and decay until it becomes either a hated cause for revolution, or a ridiculous tourist attraction – also known as a constitutional monarchy.

Constitutional monarchy

This looks like an absolute monarchy but packs none of the punch of the real thing, like having a king or queen made of Quorn. You can tell when a monarchy has lost its power because the ruler is forced to sit politely through endless renditions of a dirge (or 'anthem') played in their honour, instead of choosing to blast a brass band to smithereens when he or she is not in the mood. While constitutional monarchs are not allowed to execute their subjects like absolute monarchs are accustomed to doing, some long-serving holders of the post have made a habit of carrying a handbag at all times, which may or may not contain a taser. I'm not saying there's definitely such a thing as a royal taser. You didn't hear that from me. It's just a rumour (that I happen to believe).

Denuded though they are, constitutional monarchs aren't completely powerless. They retain the ability to open hospital wings, watch *Countdown*, defend themselves against being called a racist on *Oprah*, protect their offspring from accusations of paedophilia, that kind of thing. Most importantly, just by existing they act as a stopper, preventing the role of a nation's head of state from falling into the tiny hands of a monstrous President. This is the main reason why many of the most forward-thinking countries on Earth (and also the United Kingdom) have systems that contain constitutional monarchies. I get your thinking on that. At the same time, if a *royal family* is the best option for a fair state, it just goes to show how curious your species really is. But for the time being it brings in a fair few tourist bucks, which I'm all for.

Autocracy

a) Rule by a single individual, except that unlike a monarchy, you don't need to be born into it. An autocracy almost always contains similar amounts of pointless pageantry to a constitutional monarchy, but there's much less of the cuddly Women's Institute feel, and more of a bare-chested, judo-throwing, spy-poisoning, state-sanctioned-doping, nation-invading vibe (I'm not naming names). Some autocrats are often also known as dictators, if they become so depraved that they can't be bothered to write anything down.

b) Rule by cars. This sounds far-fetched, I know, but keep an eye on Elon Musk. If his Teslas become sentient, that shit could get real very quickly.*

Oligarchy

Rule by the few. The good news here, if you want a job where you get to wield lots of influence, is that to be an oligarch you don't have to be born into it, and there's no particular rule on *how few* the few must be before it's no longer an oligarchy (as long as it's less than the many, you're fine). So when it comes to a choice of evil political systems, this is definitely one of the more aspirational ones.

The bad news is that oligarchs often tend to find themselves living under an autocrat. This means that while they can have access to great wealth, their life expectancy is highly unpredictable. One minute they might be a globe-trotting football club owner, the next they've accidentally, mysteriously, brutally fallen out of a balcony window, impaled themselves on a spiked railing and had their remains tidied away in a holdall. If you'd like to get to know an oligarch to ask them what it's like, simply knock on any typical front door in Mayfair or Knightsbridge. They won't be there, because they leave them empty the whole time, but

---

* I understand Mr Musk is quite litigious so allow me to emphasise that in this case the phrase 'that shit' is meant as a colloquialism, not as a suggestion that Mr Musk himself is a complete shit. Perish the thought.

they may well have you followed and you'll get to meet them soon enough.

Plutocracy

This is a curious one. Usually it is taken to mean rule by the rich, but seeing as every single ruler on Earth who has held power automatically became rich, on your planet the term is entirely redundant. Fortunately in the wider cosmos it has a second, more useful meaning, which is 'rule by the citizens of Pluto'. You might not have previously heard about this, but now that humans have demoted Pluto to the status of 'dwarf planet', believe me, one day it is going to be pushed right up your news agenda. I can report that the Plutonians are pretty damn pissed off with you lot, and that they're quite up for launching an interplanetary missile strike on you next year. Especially their leader, Plutin. He's an evil psycho with no redeeming features. But don't worry humans, you're not in imminent danger. For starters, a year for Plutonians takes 248 Earth years. And Plutonians never do anything quickly, because over there it's really bloody cold.

Bureaucracy

Another word that has two important meanings: it can refer to a system of government in which most of the important decisions are taken by officials rather than by elected representatives, or it can be a term used to describe a morass of excessively complicated administration. The United Kingdom of course is both.

Attenboroughcracy

Survival of the fittest. Nuff said.

Democracy

Aha. Now we come to the juiciest one of all. Democracy means rule by the people, or more specifically, by the mob.* Or more specifically still, by the majority of the mob. Or even more specifically still, by the majority of whichever 60 per cent of the mob can ever be bothered to turn up and take part on polling day. It's a lovely idea and I'm delighted to see that instances of democracy are still surviving on Earth, because it's such an intergalactic rarity. (Planets in your galaxy currently using it: one. Countries using it properly: nil.)

To give you an equivalent, for me to discover a planet using democracy is a bit like when humans happen upon a branch of the burger chain Wimpy: it's clearly seen better days and you're amazed it's still going, but nonetheless a bit of you still fancies a taste. The twenty-first century is proving to be a turbulent time for democracy on your world. In some quarters it's thriving like never before: I'm thinking here of the big superpowers, like *Strictly Come Dancing, Britain's Got Talent* and *Eurovision*, as well as some tiny, insignificant minnows like *The Voice*. But contrastingly, in nation states – where it was designed to work – democracy seems to be receding at an alarming rate, like the Duke of Cambridge's hair.

---

* As opposed to the Mob, which is a specific issue in southern Italy. It's a lovely part of Earth to visit. Just don't take a beloved horse with you.

Democracy's biggest weakness is the inherent problem that in an election, just occasionally, the mob can get it wrong: for instance, Donald Trump, Silvio Berlusconi, Jair Bolsonaro, Margaret Thatcher, Tony Abbott, Scott Morrison, Rodrigo Duterte, Thatcher again, Dana International, Chris Hollins,* Thatcher *again*, Jim Davidson,† Hear'Say, Michelle McManus, James Arthur and Jessie Buckley (she was robbed on that BBC *Oliver!* talent show. Or so I'm told. I wasn't on Earth at the time. And I will have nothing to do with Lord Andrew Lloyd Webber, except his demise). Like I say, *just occasionally* voters get it wrong.

As well as being dogged by public apathy and a large number of historic, electoral whoopsies like the ones I've mentioned, there's another awkward truth about modern democracy: you could sue it under the Trades Descriptions Act. Because in your British system, the people don't actually get to rule anything; no, all they get to choose is which small minority of other people should be allowed to tell them what to do for the next few years. If you think that sounds suspiciously like an oligarchy, well, you're onto something. But at least it's a legitimised form of oligarchy, and instead of the people in control being billionaires, this way most of them are only millionaires, which is much fairer. What's more, in a democracy the public are able to lightly satirise the people in power via panel shows, pithy cartoons and online parodies, which really puts the bad guys in their place and stops all forms of corruption.‡

---

* Winner of *Strictly Come Dancing* in 2009. Don't worry, I had to look him up too.
† Winner of *Celebrity Big Brother*, in its appropriately numbered thirteenth series.
‡ I'm trying to get a handle on the human rhetorical technique of sarcasm. I reckon I'm getting there.

The original version of democracy on Earth was invented by the ancient Athenians and it was much more direct. This was pure, unadulterated democracy, in which every single policy decision was made by means of a referendum. Imagine that. What could possibly go wrong? Well, the thing is, unlike the Brits who had a national meltdown after just three plebiscites in a decade, by holding countless referenda* all the time the Athenians had a chance to get the hang of it. They were given the chance to vote on everything, from declarations of war to who should have to pick up the rubbish from the streets around the docks. That's right, dear reader, the ancient Athenians took bins seriously, and that's why their democracy worked. Incidentally, the name they gave to these attendants who had to clear up all the muck was the *koprologoi*, a word which translates into English as 'the Poo Men', and into Recyclonese as 'Vote Leave'.

The United Kingdom's most famous Prime Minister, Winston Churchill, once summed up parliamentary democracy as being 'the worst form of government – except for all the others that have been tried'. And Winnie was right. Because on this planet the best form never has been tried, which is just to give me power over the whole damned omniverse and leave me to it. And that's my ultimate goal, I'm not going to lie. Now some people might read that and think, 'Hang on a minute, your excellency. That sounds an awful lot like autocracy. How would you counter that accusation, Count Binface?' My answer is simple…

---

* You say referendums, I say referenda. Let's call the whole thing off – is what should have been the mantra in 2016.

My conclusion: Binocracy

Rule by bins. This form of government is utopian, glorious, infallible and tidy. As opposed to bin fires, which is what you have now. A Binocracy would be different and better than any other system for one important reason: I'm great.

Political Systems
The Count Binface À La Carte Menu

Secondi
i.e. How to Spread the Bread

So far we've looked at all the different options for who holds power. Now it's time to weigh up the options for what you can do *with* power. Again there are plenty of answers. And one correct one.

Communism

What could be better than sharing everything equally? If you're mega-rich then the answer to this is 'Quite a lot of things, actually', but calm down, don't get your Harrods knickers in a twist. I only meant it as a rhetorical question. Communism is an idea that sounds great in theory but in practice turns into an unholy mess. Like Mick Jagger and David Bowie doing 'Dancing in the Street'. And that's because there's one crimp in the plan when it comes to implementing communism: humans. So bad are they at executing this idea that they always, without fail, end up executing lots of humans instead. The reason for this is because, deep down, some people have trouble computing the idea of sharing. So much so that if any country calls itself 'the People's Republic of' somewhere, you can be 100 per cent sure that it doesn't belong to the people.

Why does it always go wrong? Let's imagine that communism is an all-you-can-eat salad cart at your local Harvester. Sure, it's great in principle, but by the time you get there you invariably find that there are no bacon bits left, someone's nicked the Thousand Island dressing, and children are throwing croutons across the restaurant at each other as rudimentary missiles. In other words, it quickly descends into chaos. So, in order to keep order, there has to be a salad cart attendant. This settles things down for a while. But, as the old saying goes, 'Who guards the Bacon Bits guard?' Before long, the attendant realises his power and he decides to start keeping back a tub of bacon bits for himself. To the customers he impulsively hands out only measly portions of bacon bits (rash rations of rashers), and he only does that if they've behaved well and built enough tractors. Meanwhile he persuades other salad cart attendants to keep quiet by bribing them with large hauls of bacon bits, leading to a dangerous situation where a small cabal of attendants owns all the bacon bits. Meanwhile the poor majority of repressed customers are soon reduced to sharing between them three kernels of sweetcorn, two circles of dried cucumber and a bit of iceberg lettuce that's past its best. It's not a recipe for happiness.

To be fair to communism, it doesn't always follow that model, and to suggest that it does would be a trifle simplistic. Sometimes it goes like this instead. Nobody gets any bacon bits unless they join the Bacon Party. Those who don't join must toil in the Harvester for little or no reward, while loyal Bacon Party members move up the chain of command, gaining pork privileges as they strive for a position inside the elite Politbutcher. A gulf quickly grows between the haves and the have-nots until one day, in protest against the party, there is a Bacon Uprising in the restaurant, which is swiftly crushed like ice from the unlimited drinks dispenser and banned from being mentioned. Stung by this close call, the Bacon Party realises that in order to survive they need to embrace market forces. From this point on bacon bits are shared *slightly* more generously among the customers, and public opinion of the Party improves. Just to be on the safe side, though, anyone who says anything bad about bacon is rounded up in the middle of the night and never heard of again spends the next twenty years at a voluntary cured meat re-education camp of their own accord. And to avoid customers getting any other ideas, the internet is not available inside the Harvester, except for a tightly controlled set of censored websites. These are accessible via the wi-fi code 'PeoplesInternet'.

Whichever of these two models prevails, either way you can be sure there's going to be a long and unpleasant arms race with the Toby Carvery over the road. Now, there will always be some voices on Earth and other planets who, despite all evidence to the contrary, will contest my analysis and claim that 'the thing about communism is that nobody's ever tried it properly'. This is proof that communists should be treated precisely the same way as bacon: i.e. cured.

Communism in a nutshell: We're all in it together. Until we kill you.

Socialism

Just like with communism, the principle of socialism sounds lovely and valid: in this system everyone has an equal share of everything, but instead of being controlled by the state, so natural is this state of affairs that there's no need for a 'state', because everyone is so happy and good at doling out everything equally among themselves. Like so many political theories it sounds like a good idea at first, but the reality is often a horror show that everyone would just like to wish away. Like a *Ghostbusters* sequel. In practice socialism tends to be a watered-down version of communism: like orange squash, it's certainly better for being diluted and it can be shared out among plenty of people, but ultimately it still tastes like Negworm piss.*

There's an important distinction to be made here, between governments who call themselves socialist and socialist opposition parties who claim to offer a progressive alternative to right-wing governments. Across not just Earth but the entire history of deep space, every socialist government shares a key characteristic: they're not so much socialist as a command economy run by a bunch of vicious gangsters (Lamda III, I'm looking at you).

But when it comes to opposition politicians who have offered voters a dreamy socialist vision, like Jeremy Corbyn, you can't throw such a stinging criticism. And that's for the simple reason

---

* Or so I'm told.

that poor old Bewilderbeard Jezza never got within a parsec of power to be able to disprove his own crazy theories. Bless him.

NB. Socialism *the actual thing* is not to be confused with 'socialism' *the casual slur*, which is something that right-wing capitalists and newspaper owners like to hurl at anyone who dares to suggest redistributing a single space credit of wealth from those who have it to those who don't. Being able to spot the difference between the two concepts is not technically difficult, but it has proved to be beyond the ken of billions of humans, helping to explain the success of conservative parties across Earth.

Champagne socialism

The tag champagne socialism is generally believed to have started in the 1990s with Tony 'I'm a pretty straight kinda guy' Blair, but I've looked into it and I can reveal that it was being used almost a century earlier as an insult to trash Ramsay MacDonald in the 1920s. This proves that New Labour wasn't really quite so new after all. Rather, it would be more accurate to label the Blair/ Brown years as Recycled Labour, and Keir Starmer's fightback as Re-Recycled Labour. In the current considerate age you'd think they might want to make more of that, but strangely they don't seem to be up for it. Their loss. It'd have the added benefit of being one step closer to Recyclon Labour, which sounds much better – and which is their inevitable fate.

As for what champagne socialism means, it's a catch-all phrase on Earth used to describe a more moderate, pragmatic wave of centre-left thinking. Just like everything on the left of politics, large movements quickly splinter into smaller factions and sub-factions, and champagne socialism has evolved into an umbrella term for a wide range of groupings, including the Bollinger Bolsheviks, Moët Mensheviks, Lambrusco Lefties, Cava Commies, Schloer Stalinists (for non-alcoholic radicals and radical non-alcoholics) and the newest tribe, the Organic Vegan English Sparkling Wine Snowflakes. If these disparate rabbles can bury their differences and form a Prosecco Progressive Alliance, they might stand a chance of taking power, because deep down most of them stand for pretty much the same thing: 'We're capitalists, really, but cuddly ones who once gave twenty quid to Greenpeace and, oh, you simply must read Marina Hyde's latest piece in the *Guardian*.'

Capitalism

This is the big one for most Earth-based readers of this book, not least because it explains the book's very existence: it's thanks to capitalism that you've bought it instead of borrowing it from the local library, and it's thanks to you from me for doing that. However, it's also thanks to the magic of capitalism that the UK book market is flooded with cynical cash-ins by fourth-rate celebrities,* which means that while by rights I should currently be celebrating a bestselling triumph by buying myself a fancy new starship, in reality I'll be lucky if the profits are enough to pay

---

* The sheer bloody cheek of them.

for a new lid for my bin, after the last one got run over on Tower Bridge on my way home from the mayoral election.[*]

Under capitalism, some people own nice things and other poorer people want nice things. To take advantage of this, some of the people with nice things then sell nice things to the other people. This makes the poorer people feel better and the rich people richer (the things being sold are almost always slightly less good than the really nice things that the people with the nice things have).

Capitalism is often seen as being diametrically opposed to communism and socialism, but historically it tends to have one identical effect, which is the creation of an exclusive echelon of the super-rich. But in capitalist societies on any planet you can always spot these individuals, because whereas the middle classes like to spend big on clothes and appearance, the super-rich choose to dress terribly, like they've just crawled out of a skip (or if they can't find a skip, a Primark). They do this as they're so rich that they not only don't need to make a good impression but actively enjoy making a bad impression.

Thus when Mr Zuckerberg shows up on a screen, either on Earth or his home world Noamaytz, and you see him wearing a pathetic T-shirt and a bizarre child's haircut, he's taunting you. And not in a meta way.

---

[*] True story.

Responsible capitalism

See champagne socialism (above). This is another way of describing the mildly dilute form of capitalism favoured by members of the centre-left brigade, such as Ed 'the Destroyer' Miliband. On Earth you are a responsible capitalist if you're one of those people who'd like to see rich bastards being taxed more but you also quite enjoyed watching *Wall Street** (in the Sigma Quadrant, you're a responsible capitalist if you buy your lasers from me).

Blairism

A byword for slightly less responsible capitalism, named after Tony Blair, who is a very rare human indeed. He reminds me of Nibloz the Vain, Viceroy of the Inzari, who similarly managed to reach the unusual position of being hated by those on his own side even more than by his opponents. (Eventually Nibloz retired and set up a Cosmic Foundation, which to this day goes around the Gamma Quadrant trying to help resolve conflicts. It has a 100 per cent record of making things worse.) To define Blairism: it is very much a Labour concept rather than a Conservative one, but only by the width of a single molecule of graphene. It also stands for the phenomenon of doing a great deal of good while in power but then pissing away every drop of respect by being an unstoppable, money-making shit.

---

* And indeed the Wolf thereof.

Brownism

A shorthand term for the fag-end of Blairism, when there's no money left.* It also means not being given a fair crack of the whip, after you've spent the best part of ten years trying to yank the whip away from the last guy and helping to ruin his go too.

Thatcherism

If Blairism is an Olympic weightlifter, then Thatcherism is a North Korean Olympic weightlifter pumped full of steroids, testosterone and propaganda, who achieves a stunning haul of gold despite trampling over all kinds of rules, precedents, customs and nor-malcy, and by the time they get fully found out it's too late and the damage has been done.

But there's more to Thatcherism than sheer, naked greed and destroying the concept of society. There's also the fun, knock-about cosplay element, which in more recent times has been picked up with alacrity by Foreign Secretary Liz Truss, who enjoys attempting to mask intellectual vacuousness with a gender-blind portrayal of Mr Benn (tip: it's not working, Liz).

---

* Not my words, the words of Liam Byrne MP, former Chief Secretary to the Treasury, who after being kicked out of power left a note for his successor reading, 'Dear Chief Secretary, I'm afraid there is no money. Kind regards – and good luck! Liam.' Some people say it with flowers; Mr Byrne said it by kindly gifting the Tories a priceless political weapon with which to bash Labour for centuries to come. As for Labour, this turn of events continues, prophetically enough, to burn.

Cameronism

The political philosophy of former British Prime Minister and PR man David 'Call Me Dave' Cameron. Opponents of Cameronism like to boil it down to the phrase 'Hug a hoodie', which he never said, while Dave's supporters prefer to highlight action on tackling poverty, which he never did. The thing is, by focusing on the things that Cameronism wasn't, both sides have a point because when it comes down to it, Cameronism means nothing at all. I'm only an alien passing through your solar system so I might be wrong but, as far as I can tell, this concept stands for nothing other than a vapid rebranding exercise to detoxify the Tory Party and copy the Blair playbook for capturing the centre ground.

What's amusing to me, and must be lamentable for humans, is that it kinda worked. I'm particularly intrigued that he got away with changing the Conservative Party logo from a torch to a tree despite the fact that his environmental policies did the opposite. The vacuity at the heart of Cameronism is perhaps best symbolised by Dave's notion of 'the Big Society'. This was sold as a revolutionary positive vision but was in fact a cynical rebadging of the idea of getting people to patch up gaping holes in public services by doing stuff for free, while he and Gideon 'Call Me George' Osborne ripped the heart out of the country through a vicious and discredited policy of austerity. In other words, the whole thing was a big porky pie. With Dave, it always seems to come down to pigs. And in them, allegedly.*

---

* I have no prima facie evidence that David Cameron has ever indulged in carnal activities with a pig, dead or alive. With that fact firmly established, I hope he enjoyed my explanation of Communism.

A danger of Cameronism is its proclivity to brazenness, which can lead followers of this philosophy to push their luck too far, such as gambling your job and reputation (not to mention a nation's future) on an unnecessary and incendiary referendum. In its own way, Cameronism has been a powerful force in shaping modern politics on Earth, and so to honour its achievements, when I recently discovered a new black hole in the Sigma Quadrant I called it 'Dave' – it's a whirling vortex from which nothing can escape, not even light or hard-fought single market memberships. It sits at the heart of a dust cloud called the Chipping Nebula, and is best avoided.

Majorism

Who cares?*

Johnsonism

Now then. In this book we've already come face to bin with the blond bumshell himself, Boris Johnson, but what of his philosophy? What does Johnsonism mean? Or rather, what did it mean, now that his political career has been hilariously vaporized? Well, of course, the answer is that it can mean absolutely anything except the truth. It's a blanket term that covers a multitude of sins, with underlying traits including incompetence, congenital lying, wilfully breaking rules (even if you've set them), changing

---

* I do, as it happens. On page 160 I shall explain my ingenious plan to harness this bizarre concept to positive effect.

course whenever it suits you, an admittedly above-average ability to entertain on satirical television panel shows, and a penchant for hiding in a fridge when the going gets tough. Digging deeper into Johnsonism – which I've done to save you the grisly displeasure – I have discovered that it appears to entail a psychological state of being in which one spends his or her entire life being hellbent on pursuing a job that they are woefully ill equipped to do, while all the time pretending that they're not interested, and treating public life as a schoolboy game to be sniggered through in between parties at oligarchs' mansions and dinners at the Garrick Club.

NB. This doctrine won a landslide majority in a UK general election.

Related to this unfortunate phenomenon is boosterism, which has a double meaning. In outer space it refers to putting actual boosters on things to make them go faster. Under Johnsonism, it was a giant exercise in trying to distract voters from how bad things are, and involved peacocking about in high-vis vests while talking in florid, upper-class gobbledegook about 'levelling up', with a childish smirk on your face that betrayed the fact you didn't give a shit about the north. For a precise parallel, imagine a clown at a house party making a balloon poodle while the entire house is on fire, due to an incident an hour earlier in which a house fire was started by a clown. That's Johnsonian Boosterism.

Fortunately, as with everything, there's a flipside to Johnsonism: it can also refer to a delicious concept in politics where you think you've won a plum job which will be lots of fun and contain endless privileges, but which turns out to mean dealing with wars, pandemics, numerous scandals of your own making, Cabinet colleagues plotting against you and all the very worst that life can bring, showing you up for the hopeless prong you truly are.

Euphemism

See Johnsonism.

Liberalism

People who want to be free to be an individual.

Libertarianism

People who want to be free to be an idiot.

Corbynism

Socialism + Libertarianism + Optimism + Anti-Semitism = Corbynism.

My conclusion: Countbinism

Do whatever I say and everything will be cool.

Part Four

The State of Your Nation

Part Four

The State of Your Nation

I pledge that electing Count Binface as Earth's first alien leader, on a platform of unprecedented modernisation, will drag the tired and creaking mechanisms of the British Isles out of the Eighties (the 1680s, in many cases) and into the present. Naturally, when the next election comes along, it goes without saying that all the human opposition parties will make this same promise too. But unlike some 'official' opposition figureheads, I don't just talk the talk (in a slight adenoidal rasp, as recent Labour leaders seem prone to do) or rely on an admittedly strong general vibe of not being Boris. I am all that *and more*, thanks to my uniquely bold set of constitutional reforms.

To help pave the way for my inevitable landslide electoral triumph, I have carried out a thorough assessment of the state of your nation (seriously guys, the state of your nation!), and I've identified a few areas that could do with a teeny-weeny bit of sprucing up. The vast array of ancient institutions that make the UK tick are a complex patchwork, and politicians know that they tinker with it at their peril. Unless they're me. I'm fortunate to be unshackled by the usual concerns about unpicking Britain's fragile political system, because it's not my planet so I've got absolutely nothing to lose. Therefore in this chapter, exclusively for you, dear reader, I present for the first time my full, comprehensive guide to overhauling the fusty and rusty apparatus of the British constitution. Behold some of the delicious, (r)evolutionary* ways in which I plan to shake things up.

The royal family

We covered the general role of royal families in Chapter Three, insomuch as they act as a kind of sparkly, hoity-toity Polyfilla – blocking up a constitutional gap so that you don't need to elect a president. As for the UK's specific royal family, the Windsors, I know what you're thinking: 'Now that you're here, Count Binface, we don't need them. Bin 'em!' That's very kind of you, dear reader, but I should make it clear on the record that I am not looking to exterminate the royals. I merely wish to solidify their ceremonial role so that they become the living, breathing version of Madame Tussauds that deep down the public wants. Incidentally, each year the royal family costs the British tax-payer £69.4million,† which is slightly less than a family day ticket to Madame Tussauds.

Everyone knows that the royal family has been through years of crisis, so much so that Prince Edward is now seen as a safe

---

* Evolution and revolution are the same thing: it's just a question of speed. Some things work better when they go fast, while others need to go a bit slower. Like the difference between vinyl singles and LPs. Or between most lawyers and Dominic Raab.

† According to the Sovereign Grant accounts, 2020.

pair of hands. Are they beyond hope? Or can their reputation yet be salvaged, despite the unfortunate fact of Prince Charles becoming the next king? I believe I have their ticket to redemption. My first suggestion is a pledge that I first made in my blockbusting 2021 London mayoral manifesto, with regard to royal accommodation. I've got nothing against the Windsors having a palace in the Earth capital. Bully for them. But four? Three too* many. So I say that they can keep one of Buckingham Palace, Kensington Palace, St James's Palace and Clarence House (their choice – I'm nice like that), and the rest will be gifted to the nation to help eradicate homelessness. If the royals should complain that one palace in the capital isn't enough (remember, I'm letting them hang onto Windsor, Balmoral and Sandringham too), then they will be forced to buy a holding stake in Crystal Palace FC. No less an expert than Gary Lineker declared on Twitter that this pledge was 'interesting', and he's right. It is. Because this should be in *every* party manifesto. Does it really take a space warrior to say it's indefensible that a wealthy nation like the UK should allow anyone to sleep rough on the streets, and that for this to happen in the shadow of gigantic empty palaces isn't just illogical but obscene? Does it really take an alien to ask what could be better than having all Trooping the Colour pageants replaced with a display by Croydon's finest cheerleading group, the Palace Crystals? Vote for me and all of this will happen.

---

* A little rhetorical flourish there for GCSE English students to pick up on.

In terms of royal family personnel, I would do what fellow alien Rylan does with his beard and indulge in a bit of stylish and targeted pruning. If you ask me, Queen Elizabeth II deserves every credit for her remarkable job in sitting on the throne for seventy years,* and I appreciate that the Windsors always need to have an heir. So Kate and Wills, have no fear, I shan't be packing you, Georgie Porgie and the gang off to a JobCentre Plus, except perhaps to open one now and then. But I've got a sneaky feeling that just a few of the royals could be gently nudged out and forced to live like ordinary citizens. Just a few. Say, for instance, the Duke and Duchess of Kent, Princess Alexandra, the Duke and Duchess of Gloucester, Beatrice and Eugenie, Prince and Princess Michael of Kent, Princess Alexandra, Zara Phillips and Mike Tindall, Peter and Autumn Phillips, Lady Sarah Chatto, Lord Freddie Windsor, Lady Gabriella Windsor, Lady Louise Windsor, Viscount Severn, the Earl of Snowdon, the Earl of Ulster, Lady Helen Taylor, Lady Davina Elizabeth Alice Benedikte Windsor, and Lady Rose Victoria Birgitte Louise Gilman. Just a few. There are twenty-four non-royal dukes out there too – Norfolk, Bedford, Somerset, Richmond, Grafton, Richmond, Westminster and so on. They can also go in the bin. Down with the dukes. Up with the Count!

There are still a couple of high-profile figures I've yet to

---

* Elsewhere in the galaxy only Nibloz the Vain can match that achievement, and that was a truly terrible case of constipation.

mention, the most notorious being the Duke of York. I think the fairest thing to do to this tosspot by royal appointment is to keep the scumbag to his word. So listen up, Randy Andy: if you can eat a punnet of Scotch Bonnet chillies without producing a single bead of sweat, while sitting in front of a blast furnace (which I'm willing to supply), then you should be cleared of all suspicion and your good name should be reinstated at the top of British society. If you should produce one molecule of perspiration, then it's the Phantom Zone for you, sunshine. Or the furnace. Up to you, Andy. That's democracy.

As for Prince Harry, he has left the royal family (and his Nazi-costume-wearing youth) behind him to start a new career as a podcaster and influencer, and I say good for him. I would particularly like to congratulate him on finding a fine match. I once worked with Mega Marksman to quell an uprising on Sigma VI. She's a great gal, and an even greater shot. One blast from her plasma rifle is enough to make mincemeat out of a tubby former tabloid editor. She's not to be trifled with lightly.

Fixing Parliament – literally

The Palace of Westminster is currently undergoing much-needed renovation work, in a process that's set to take thirty years and cost somewhere between £4- and 6 billion. (Fact fans: the Poles refurbished their parliament building in six weeks for 2,000 euros, cash in hand. And it's better than ever.) The price of the British upgrade sounds a bit steep to me, but once I'm in power I'm prepared to continue the investment on one condition: that the money is used to upgrade the hallowed estate *properly*. IMHO the following enhancements are non-negotiable:

The famous green benches of the House of Commons must be fitted with small retractable spikes, which can emerge through the upholstery when required. This is to wake up MPs if they fall asleep, for the improvement of debates; and to lightly impale Jacob Rees-Mogg even if he doesn't, for banter purposes alone.

The dispatch box should do what it says on the tin, and eject from the premises any minister who spouts a lie, sending them rocketing through a specially designed hatch in the roof. This will be called the Dispatch Hatch. And it will be sponsored by Ronseal, to rake in a bit of cash.

There shouldn't be a speaker in the middle of the House of Commons. This is the twenty-first century. There should be four, with one in each corner, to quadraphonically keep control of the loud, boorish (inevitably male) members who continually misbehave and abuse their position (not to mention the staff). 'Order, Order'? I give you Fourder, Fourder!

The mace (or the big gold stick that sits in the middle of the Commons, if you want to get technical) is gaudy and ridiculous. It doesn't even contain a laser. What's the point of it? It should be sold to raise money for the homeless, and replaced by a chocolate one covered in gold wrapping paper, which can be eaten by whichever party wins the next election.

Black Rod's garden entrance to be used only by those aged sixteen and over.

At the front of the Palace, where there are currently pegs for members to hang up their swords, there should also be room for laser docks so I can charge my lightsabre.*

A holodeck should be installed on the ground floor of the building, so that politicians can experience real life in all its different forms via holographic projections, enabling them to make better decisions for the good of the nation. This will also deny them the claptrap excuse they always splutter about why it's useful for them to take a cushy, lucrative second job in the private sector, when they're already earning a big fat salary from taxpayers. NB. This new holodeck is not to be confused with a hollow deck, which is what they have at present.

Stella Creasy MP has done great work in promoting the updating of antiquated traditions to allow members who are mothers to have the right to carry out their work. I would like to take this further and introduce a parliamentary soft play area, which would be a dedicated place for elderly MPs to go where they can be distracted without hurting themselves, so that they're no longer a nuisance to the young mothers in Parliament who are trying to get some legislation done.

All public subsidies of bars and restaurants in the Palace of Westminster would be stopped on day one of a Binface government. Taxpayers shouldn't be paying for MPs to get pissed during working hours, and to be blunt, MPs shouldn't be paying for that either. They're supposed to be doing a fucking job. So the bars will only be open from 1 to 2 p.m. and 6 to 11 p.m. During

---

* My publishers tell me that the word 'lightsabre' may be subject to copyright, which as you'll know is something that these days I'm very sensitive to. Thus I have coined the term 'photon epée' as a replacement, just in case.

the intervening hours, these spaces will instead be hired out for life drawing classes, Weight Watchers and zumba. Putting some money *back* in the public purse.

A Laser Quest would be good (for after-work zapping only, of course).

There is currently a big problem inside the halls of Westminster with rats. Especially chatty ones. To stop these, more CCTV will be placed in stationery cupboards and other likely spots for clandestine assignations by former health secretaries.

Finally, experts predict that while the Palace of Westminster is being refitted it will be far cheaper if Parliament is temporarily moved to an alternative location during the works than if it continues to operate in the middle of a building site. Speaking personally, I'm someone who hasn't had enough of experts, so I would listen to their wisdom and insist that members use a new debating chamber until their famous old home is restored. It will be essential for British MPs to continue to meet in a venue at the heart of international affairs, and at a location which has cheaper rent than Westminster, making Brussels the obvious choice.

Fixing Parliament – figuratively

Sorting out the bricks and mortar of crumbly old Westminster is the easy bit. Now we need to roll up our armoured sleeves and consider the trickier conundrum of the legislators themselves. But I'm pretty sure I've hit upon a recipe to spruce up the calibre of MPs. To begin with, I say that all MPs' pay should be tied to that of nurses for the next 100 years. 'You can't do that!'

politicians will scream. 'That will put off the brightest and best from entering Parliament,' they will screech. To which I will reply, 'Human testicles.'* I say it will have a startlingly positive effect for this reason: never in the history of British politics have MPs willingly voted to cut their own pay, so my measure will have the natural effect of massively boosting nurses' salaries to match. And if any Member of Parliament wants to argue that their job is harder than the average sister's, then I will force them to take a night shift at Lewisham Hospital A&E unit for the next fifty-two Saturdays, to see if that changes their mind.

When it comes to sorting out Parliament, it would be remiss of your new Recyclon overlord if I didn't take the opportunity to clean up the place and bin the stench of corruption that has long dogged the Westminster village. Which brings me to the 'Ministerial Code'. This is a strange set of rules which MPs often accuse each other of breaking, but which never seems to result in adequate punishment. Like Thierry Henry committing an outrageous handball and France still going to the World Cup at Ireland's expense. It's as if the House of Commons is a pirate ship and the code comprises guidelines more than actual rules. This needs sorting out. I demand that all breaches of the Ministerial Code should be judged by the UK Supreme Court (of which I should be a member, obviously). This would end the ludicrous practice of politicians marking their own homework and of the Prime Minister being accountable only to himself or herself. My new

---

* Is that idiomatic? Or at times like this must one specifically use the word 'bollocks'? Either way, you catch my drift.

rule would be applied retrospectively, dating back to the start of the Johnson premiership – so Bozza, if you're reading this, you'll be firmly in the crosshairs whatever you're up to at that point. Just because you've been ignominiously turfed out of Downing Street doesn't make you safe from me. Them's the breaks. And just to maintain the piratical theme, a plank will be fitted to the Commons Terrace that overlooks the River Thames, so that any MP or ex-MP found guilty can be forced to walk it. These events would be broadcast free-to-air as they happen for all to see. Now that's what I call a live stream.

Fixing Parliament – electorally

It's one thing cleaning up the acts of those lucky few humans who get to call Parliament their place of 'work'. But it's arguably even more important to sort out who is getting elected there in the first place. When you want a wash, you want your shower to be hooked up to the clean water supply rather than a raw sewage pipe. So I can't for the life of me work out why British democracy seems intent on doing the opposite. If you're happy with the status quo, of course, go ahead and vote for one of the 'mainstream' loser parties. But if you want something different, and relatively sane, strap in for some laser-guided common sense.

Let's start with the basics. On Sigma IX we have a little rule for choosing rulers: they have to actually live in the place they want to govern. (We also have an even better rule, which is that they should be me.) Seems pretty straightforward, wouldn't you say? But the UK has no such principle. The reason for this is so that the mainstream parties can parachute favoured candidates into safe seats when a juicy vacancy turns up, but I say let's take away the parachutes! Ever since my first manifesto in 2017, I have pledged that all parliamentary candidates should have lived in the constituency they wish to represent for five years prior to the election (apart from Luton North, in which case you're allowed to commute). That way, each local area would be sending a representative who knows the vicinity to speak for them in Parliament rather than having someone foisted upon them from the Earth capital who has no clue about the region, the people or the normal way of life, nor any empathy whatsoever. Or 'Etonians' for short. Adopting my new measure, which must be called the Binface Amendment, could of course limit the opportunities for a space warrior from the Sigma Quadrant to serve as an MP, but that just goes to show how principled I am. And anyway, I'm pretty sure the British people will be happy to leave a loophole open and grant me a special exemption to stand against the Prime Minister of the day. Is all of this far-fetched? Guys, if Baron Evgeny Lebedev of Hampton and Siberia can get a parliamentary pass, anything's possible.

Another little tweak which I humbly suggest will improve the quality of MPs is to amend the voting system at general elections. Currently the UK uses the 'first past the post' system, so called because it is weighted to make sure that the same people usually finish first, and because on the rare occasions when that doesn't happen they like to blame voting by post. I have to tell you that Earth is the only planet in the omniverse which has ever contained life forms who think that democracies are best elected using first past the post. Every other world that has flirted with the wonders of democracy quickly upgraded to a more sophisticated method of voting: a type of proportional representation called the Appropriate Victor, or AV for short. Now, I know that there's a problem with this in the UK because it has the same initials as the 'alternative vote' system which was proposed by Sir Nick Clegg in 2011 and defeated in a public vote. And to be honest, it's not just the initials that are the same. It's the same system. The problem is simply that on Earth its main advocate was Mr Clegg, so it was doomed from the start.

Why do I like AV? Well, a version of it was used in the Earth capital's 2021 mayoral election for one thing, and once second preferences were included, it increased the total number of votes I won from 24,775 to 92,896. In other words, it magnifies greatness. If it were used at a future general election, it would free up every constituent – regardless of their political hue – to vote for the Count Binface Party as their first choice, in protest at how poorly run the country is – and then to choose one of the human contestants as their second choice. Now you might read this and think, 'That's all well and good but if everyone registered a protest vote like that, Count Binface, you'd end up winning.' Precisely.

By the way, don't think I haven't noticed that since my mayoral moral triumph, a bill has been quietly passed at Westminster which changes the rules for future London elections, replacing AV with a simple first past the post vote. Why have they snuck through this disgraceful amendment? Simple: I've got 'em worried. And they should be worried. Whatever the system, solar or electoral, I shall be victorious.

Critics of proportional representation argue that it is more likely to lead to hung Parliaments. I'd argue that this in itself would not hinder responsible government if MPs were able to work constructively together. The problem is that recent instances of the phenomenon have been not-very-well-hung parliaments. Unless you believe the rumours about Michael Gove.

Sorry, can you give me a moment? I just need to take a break from writing while I bleach that thought from my memory banks. I'll be back on the next page.

Sorry about that. Right, where was I? Ah, yes. Hung parliaments. And Michael Gove. No, it's no good. The image is still
there. Let me just refresh my memory banks again.

That's better. Let's move onto the next topic.

Devolution and referenda

We don't have devolution on Sigma IX. Logically this phenomenon should denote the opposite of evolution, and politically
speaking I assume it means the act of regressing into a state of
unsophistication and idiocy. Is that an appropriate name for what
the United Kingdom has done to its own government? You tell
me. I couldn't possibly comment. All I can say is that from an
alien's viewpoint, devolution is pretty clearly a gateway drug to
regional independence/national destruction (take your pick).
Being a big fan of democracy on your planet, ultimately I think
that the humans of each nation of the UK should have the right
to choose their fate. But while I'm all in favour of increasing
freedoms, I have a sneaky feeling that if your species keeps on
dividing, it might – just might – end up becoming counterproduc-
tive. First Britain splits from Europe. Then Scotland from Britain.
Then Glasgow from Scotland. Then the Southside from Glasgow.
Then number 1 Acacia Road from the rest of the street. Then Mrs
Eileen McTavish from the rest of number 1 Acacia Road. Then
the hairy mole on the side of Eileen's left cheek from the rest of
Mrs McTavish. It could all get a bit silly. One need only look at
my own (very welcome) support from the 'Dorset Independence
Party' for proof of that. Still, as long as each decision is reached
by a free and fair vote, there's no reason each question shouldn't
be asked.

But *how often* should you 'ask the audience'? Chris Tarrant did it once or twice a show. The Swiss do it twice a year. (But Switzerland only let women have the vote as late as Earth year 1971, so they're not an ideal example.) On Sigma IX we like to take a more thoughtful, calibrated approach based on impeccable Recyclon logic, and this came in very handy during my 2017 election campaign on Earth against Theresa May. While the Maybot struggled to come up with a coherent Brexit deal, and the Labour Party couldn't work out whether they were for Leave or Remain, I offered a simple and effective solution: there should be another referendum, about whether there should be another referendum. It made perfect sense. Sadly the humans chose another course – one that ended up with Boris Johnson in charge. I'll leave you to decide which eventuality was healthier for democracy.

At the time of writing, the question of independence is bubbling up once again in Scotland. The ruling SNP, led by Nicola Sturgeon, claims that they should have a right to hold an IndyRef2 because Brexit has caused 'a material change in circumstances' since IndyRef1 was held in 2014. I quite agree, and I support the Nationalists' call for a fresh vote. Surely both sides have nothing to be scared of, seeing as their case is so unequivocally strong? However, I do have a small proviso. Should the 'yes' campaign win next time round, it will cause a material change in circumstances that will simply have to be addressed by another referendum. Fair's fair.

While I like the idea of referenda in principle, there's a good reason why I'm cautious about them in practice. That's because before I first travelled to Earth in 2017, I had only recently just finished quelling an Oddurm insurrection on Sigma X. What had happened was that a tiny hardcore of Oddurms, led by a rogue element called Farkanfaraj, had got the idea into their heads that they didn't need to be part of the Sigma Union any more and they'd be better off going it alone. I know, I know, it sounds mad. But contrary to expectation, they managed to convince a very small majority of the population (I think it was about 51.8 per cent) to support the idea of leaving our solar system, because apparently the rest of us were 'holding them back'. This was a crisis that called for real leadership if disaster was to be averted, so I took the immediate decision not to sod off on a three-week holiday until it was all over. Instead I hyperjumped to Sigma X and tried to explain to the Oddurms that yes, the rest of the system was indeed holding them back, but only gravitationally. I pointed out that without the fundamental force of gravity holding it in orbit, Sigma X would drift off into deep space with no star to heat it and no access to the Sigma market (which I'm proud to say is the largest single trading bloc in the Virgo supercluster). The Oddurm separatists wouldn't be swayed by these rational arguments so I came up with a compromise. On the one hand I granted full citizenship on Sigma IX to the 48.2 per cent who wished to remain, along with the retention of their Union membership. On the other hand I allowed the 51.8 per cent to exercise their right to take their planet and leave if they so wished. And they did. Sigma X was duly untethered from its orbit and it has now floated two parsecs away from the rest of the system into independence. According to the latest reports it's also a frozen inhospitable nightmare. But to be fair to those Oddurms who live there, they do have their sovereignty back, as well as some shiny commemorative coins. Not only that, but they're now free to form gravitational orbits with any other star they choose, even if it'll take them several million years to reach one. If all that sounds like your idea of a good time, you're welcome to visit Sigma X. They offer temporary visas for outlanders to pick their spacewort harvest, for our financial equivalent of 1p per week. Nobody's yet taken them up on that offer, strangely enough. As for what happened to Farkanfaraj? After the vote, he immediately applied for citizenship on my planet of Sigma IX. His application was rejected, and he currently resides in the Phantom Zone.

Don't let this cautionary tale put you off the idea of increasing democracy, though. There is as ever a third way in intergalactic politics, one that charts a course between centralised control from a single capital on the one hand and the potential difficulties of breaking away from successful unions on the other. This is to have 'Devolution in Name Only', or DINO, as I call it, and it's what Michael [I'm shuddering as I type the name] Gove sneakily planned to roll out as part of his 'Levelling Up Agenda'. The only thing that Govey has ever levelled up to my knowledge are his own endorphins after a quick sniff of party powder, but still, the cunning little scrote has nearly worked this bit of politicking out. It's a more fashionable, zeitgeisty and vacuous way to do devolution, and involves the creation of a host of new mayors across the country. The trend started in 2000 with the first elected mayor for the Earth capital, London, a post that has been held by Ken Livingstone, Boris Johnson and Sadiq Khan. So it's not a hard job, clearly, and it will be mine – all mine – come 2024 (or worst case scenario 2028). But now the trend is going nationwide. The Tories are showering new mayoralties all over the land like giant lizard droppings. To show you what I mean, in 2022 even Croydon gained its first directly elected mayor, despite being a borough of London, which already has a mayor.* Where will the new rash of anointed local figureheads end? How many Andy Burnhams does it take to change a northern transport policy? And will these new regional politicians undermine the traditional role of local MPs? Some experts would suggest that these new mayoralties are too numerous, too expensive and too pointless. But that's like poor old King Cnut trying to hold back the tide. The real problem is there still aren't enough of them. I recommend that the UK should go the whole hog and keep going until they have created 650 mayors, with each one representing a small amount of territory. Then, get this, they could all meet in a central location for regular debates and to take votes on how to improve the country. They could have some kind of 'Common House', where they could all get together, maybe in the capital city. Is that crazy? Maybe it'd never work.

---

* Incidentally, the decision to have a Croydon mayor was adopted after a referendum that attracted a turnout of only 21 per cent. The few locals who did bother to cast a ballot chose by a ratio of four to one to reject the pre-existing council structure, which had scandalously bankrupted the borough. In its place, according to the website Inside Croydon, voters opted for 'change to a directly elected mayor, or something that is #ABitLessShit'.

The honours system

The knighthood. Britain's gold standard accolade, awarded to subjects who through the centuries have displayed exceptional ability and valour. Sir Lancelot, Sir Walter Raleigh, Sir Francis Drake, Sir Isaac Newton, to name but a few. And then we come to more recent times. Sir Fred Goodwin, Sir Mark Thatcher, Sir Jimmy Savile, Sir Rolf Harris, Sir Clement Freud. It's hard to avoid the conclusion that a serious amount of grade inflation has been going on, never better proven than by the elevation of – and I can't quite believe this was allowed – *Sir* Gavin Williamson. Therefore when I am in power I shall immediately review the honours system and all knighthoods handed out due to party donations or political favour will be rescinded and recycled, handed out instead to primary care workers who worked their surgical socks off during the Covid pandemic.

As for the messy range of badges and baubles that make up the rest of the honours system, I'd abolish the lot, with one exception. I'd keep the MBE – for Members of the Binface Empire – and immediately start dishing them out to the *crème de la crème* of human society in the UK. And to set the ball rolling, here, exclusively for you, dear reader, is my inaugural Binface honours list:

Members of the Binface Empire

Ian McShane (you should all know why by now)
Chris Rea (for services to music and traffic reporting)
Clive Myrie (for services to mastering news and minds)
Usain Bolt (for services to dabbing and running)

Newport Pagnell's Welcome Break (for Services)

John Craven (for services to Countryphiles, knitted jumpers and being a boss)

Gina Coladangelo (for services to removing Matt Hancock from the Cabinet)

Idris Elba (for services to acting and badassery)

Lauren Laverne (for services to music and highly erudite chat)

Marcus Rashford (for services to free school meals, social mobility and inspiring youth. Oh, and football too)

Eve Muirhead (for services to curling)

Rob Curling (for services to 1990s daytime quiz shows)

Nadiya Hussain (for services to red velvet cake)

Emily Maitlis (for services against Prince Andrew)

Peppa Pig (for services to humiliating Boris Johnson)

Taylor Swift (for services to annoying Damon Albarn)

Ros Atkins (for services to speaking actual facts with a straight face)

Anya Taylor-Joy (for services to chess and defeating Russians)

Andy Murray (for first and second service)

Joe Wicks (for services to staving off/causing insanity: delete as applicable)

Michael and Emily Eavis (for services to medieval battlefield reenactments)

John Adams (for services to inventing Ceefax)

Timmy Mallett (for no particular reason)

Volodymyr Zelensky (for services to being a total legend)

And of course the entire cast and crew of *Lovejoy* (for services to being epic).

NB. My publishers have alerted me to a problem with my honours list, in that they are suspicious that I have only included the wonderful Lauren Laverne in order to curry favour with her and get a guest spot on *Desert Island Discs*. Let me put on the record (pun intended) that nothing could be further from the truth, even though my application for the flagship interview series is already under consideration, as you can see from this Twitter conversation from January 2022, which the BBC should know is legally binding:

@BBCRadio4: Who's the best *Desert Island Discs* castaway ever?

@CountBinface: Me, in 2024.

Journalist Nick Stylianou: Can you functionally survive on a desert island?

@CountBinface: I'll keep my starship cloaked nearby just in case.

@BBCRadio4: Any use of a starship is an instant disqualification I'm afraid. The rules are very clear.

@CountBinface: You see, it's outdated thinking like this that has got Nadine Dorries licking her lips. Show me where Roy Plomley bans starships or give me my 45 mins with my good friend @LaurenLaverne.

@LaurenLaverne: *Consults the scrolls* Unless it's Jefferson Starship. In which case fill your boots.

@CountBinface: Nothing's Gonna Stop Me Now.

The House of Lords

Finally we come to the big one. The horrendously stinking one. The House of Lords. This festering piece of effrontery is the second biggest legislative chamber on planet Earth, behind the Chinese National People's Congress, and it's equally democratic. It's so big that it's the only upper house of any bicameral parliament in the omniverse that's larger than the lower house; so massive that there's no way all the members can fit inside. It's basically the least healthy entity ever to exist in a democracy. And despite the fact that they occasionally get important things right, I'm sorry but they've gotta go. And I say that even though I have personally been mentioned during a debate in the House of Lords, in a moment that was nearly as exciting as when I was mentioned during a question on Richard Osman's *House of Games*. It was Baroness Jenny Jones who raised my name in November 2021, as part of a debate about access to democracy at general elections, and I'm glad if my intergalactic wonderfulness was able to be of some assistance to her. However, it should be pointed out that while Baroness Jones has, like me, publicly called for the abolition of the Lords, this hasn't stopped her from turning up at Parliament and taking the £323 daily allowance.* Unlike me. I would have thought that if you don't think something should exist, taking cash from it is a pretty curious way to go about abolishing it.

---

* According to the UK Parliament website, in October 2021 (the month before she mentioned me) Baroness Jones of Moulsecoomb attended the Lords for thirteen days and opted to take home the full discretionary amount of £4,199 available to her.

But the UK's second chamber is home to far more egregious whoopsies than that. Let's take a moment to call out just a few of the humans who the British government has deemed fit to be made a lord: Andrew Lloyd Webber, Ian 'Beefy' Botham, Evgeny 'My dad was in the KGB but I'm alright, guv' Lebedev, Alan Sugar, Zac Goldsmith, Jo Johnson, Karren Brady, Kate Hoey, Julian Fellowes, Michael Flatley and Voldemort (I think I've got that right). My response to this list is simple. Wipe them out. All of them.

I must emphasise I'm not just saying this because I used to be a lord myself, having assumed the Buckethead title until my unfortunate battle on the planet Copyright. No way, Hose A or Hose B. Unlike Jenny Jones, this space warrior has practised what he preached and renounced his peerage. After giving up my old title, I discovered that a certain human – a pipe-toking Earthling by the name of Tony Benn – had once upon a time done the same thing. Being a bit naive about your planet at the time, I wondered if 'Tony' was an honorific title given to former lords, and on that basis I considered calling myself Tony Binface. Then I looked into recent Earth history and discovered that while Tony can refer to a Labour politician known for putting principles before power, it can also refer to a recent Labour politician known for doing the opposite.

What else is wrong with the House of Lords? I could fill a whole book just on that alone, but for brevity's sake here are just three more little issues that this alien thinks are a bit rum:

In a country that has spent decades trying to sort out a crippling social care sector, it's ironic that at the very heart of government there should be a cosy, state-sponsored, leather-upholstered, gold-embossed luxury care home. Readers, they're laughing at you.

At the time of writing (Earth year 2022), the House of Lords still contains hereditary peers. Not one or two, but ninety-two of the travesties. That's the same number as there are clubs in the four divisions of the football league, but with more Russian influence. And believe it or not, these hand-me-down lawmakers are the only members of the Lords who are chosen by election. I'm telling you, guys, they're laughing at you.

Finally, part of the membership is reserved for the 'Lords spiritual' – it sounds like a haunted house but the truth is far less fun. It refers to the twenty-six bishops who get to take a seat in the UK's second chamber and vote on legislation simply because of their place in the Church of England. This is like inviting a couple of dozen people to have a say in the laws of the land just because they're flat-Earthers. It's insane.*

To put it bluntly, Britons have had to put up with government after government and opposition after opposition promising and then failing to sort out this embarrassingly corrupt congress of crap. Only I can be counted on to bin it for good. And trust me, it'll be worth it. What the country will lose in the ceremonial rabbit-fur coat-manufacturing trade, and its centuries-old tradition of state-sponsored snoozing, you'll gain in a modicum of democratic accountability.

---

* By the way, I could have picked any number of groups there, not just the flat-Earthers. Any resemblance between an extreme faction whose beliefs are patently poppycock and the Anglican Church is entirely coincidental.

But the question is, what would fill the void and take the place of the Lords instead? You'll be pleased to know I've got just the ticket.

On Sigma IX we have an upper house of parliament. (Purely advisory, of course – just like the lower house, they all answer to me.) But we have a very cunning way to go about appointing the members, and it's something that you humans could establish quickly and easily too. It is a fact of life throughout the omniverse that many heavyweight public figures suffer defeats in their career and find themselves drenched with opprobrium during their time in the spotlight. And it is equally a fact that many of these souls accrue an unexpected veneer of wisdom and authority once they step away from frontline politics. All it takes is for them to no longer seek power and suddenly they are seen by the masses not as a useless waste of hyperspace but as a wise and grizzled elder. Not showing ambition is a very shrewd move, and I harnessed this power in my early days as leader of the Recyclons, with my wildly successful poster campaign 'Follow Count Binface. He doesn't give a shit.' (This also led me to a lucrative advertising gig as the face of intergalactic constipation treatment 'Galaxative', but I digress.) And it's something that certain humans have learned to make the most of, too. Just look at Sir John Major, Gordon Brown, William Hague and even Ed Miliband. Not so long ago they were seen as total no-hopers. And yet in the current climate they seem not half bad. The same can happen in other nations too, as one-term US President Jimmy Carter experienced when he soared beyond two-termers Bill Clinton and George W Bush in the public's esteem. We can even boil it down to an equation:

Failure x Time = Respect

What is this strange alchemy?* I don't claim to know the answer, but what I do know is that the UK needs to take advantage of it like I have. Thus I propose that the Lords should be replaced by an elected senate as the second chamber, and then on top of that there should be a *third* chamber filled with the kind of people I have described above. It will be called the House of Losers (I know the current House of Lords stands for pretty much the same thing, so you might as well make it official). Imagine a dedicated space for noble Britons who know what it is like to strive for the best and come up agonisingly short, to help point the government away from making gross mistakes. Who could advise the House of Commons better than a congregation containing the likes of Tim Henman, Eddie 'The Eagle' Edwards, the engineers of Beagle 2, Gareth Gates, Jimmy White, Liberty X, Jürgen from *The Great British Bake Off*, Johanna Konta, Elise Christie, Greg Rusedski, Gareth Southgate, Gina G, Sam Ryder – indeed all UK *Eurovision* entrants who didn't win – the 1990s England men's cricket team, the 1995–6 Newcastle United squad, the Euro 2020 England men's football team, and Ultravox.

I know that my plans will be refreshing to voters' auditory organs and alarming to the establishment in equal measure. But I have a message to mollify the fears of the crusty old so-and-sos who've been clogging up the legislature for too long: don't worry,

---

* There is always an exception that proves the rule. For an example of an unalloyed disaster as party leader who is still regarded as such, see Iain Duncan Smith.

old beans, we're not completely upsetting the apple cart – we'll make sure that the motto above the chamber door is in Latin:

Si primo loco deficis, ter quaterque conarere. Si tum demum deficies, senatui servi.

'If at first you don't succeed, try, try and try again. If you still don't, work for Parliament.'

Part Five

The Count Binface Manifesto

And now, Earthlings, we come to the main event. So far on Earth I have stood in three elections and each time I have brought out a manifesto packed with a potent mix of progressive policies that has outflanked my rivals and sent my political star rocketing (to ninth place in London). But all of that was just an *amuse-bouche*. Here, for dear readers of this volume, I am delighted to present my most comprehensive set of plans yet. Each one will transform the United Kingdom and by extension your whole planet for the better. Taken together, they are a path to the sunlit uplands. For far too long, the UK has had a government that has stripped back public spending – it's been death by a thousand cuts, with a silent 'n'. Well, not any more. It's time to tax fairly and spend hugely. It's time for Count Binface.

Think of me as an interstellar Marie Kondo – through my galactic conquests I have become an expert at organising space. And Britain is in space, so let's spruce you up.

The Binistry of Transport

You may be relieved to know that transport problems aren't only a problem on Earth. They crop up on every planet. Especially the ones with low gravity – if you ever find yourself on a world like that, don't be lulled by how fast you can walk; trust me, things can quickly (and literally) get out of hand.

I'm pleased to say that back on Sigma IX, these days things are tickety-boo transport-wise, since I took all the infrastructure back into public (i.e. my) ownership. Prior to my reforms, our transport system used to be managed privately by a race of bureaucrats called the Graylings, and a piss-poor job they did too. If you haven't heard of them, the Graylings are hairless, spineless creatures famous for being the worst administrators in hyperspace. They had a go at trying to slightly adjust our hoverbus timetables, and instead succeeded in leaving the entire population of my planet marooned – it turned out that they had outsourced rocket construction to a company that owned no rockets, had never built a rocket, and which had made all their money selling cakes. As a punishment I banished into exile the Grayling leader – named Kryz Tupha – and sent him hurtling through a wormhole so he could bother another solar system far away from mine.

As for me, some humans might wonder why I have travelled such a vast distance and come to your planet in pursuit of my political goals. But in reply I would point out that everything is relative, and the space fuel needed to cross the nine million light years between Earth and the Sigma Quadrant is in fact cheaper than a season ticket from London to Brighton.

Right now transport is one of the biggest problems facing modern Britain, and luckily it's one of the easiest to fix, too. Here are my promises. Vote for me and they shall be done.

London Bridge to be renamed Phoebe Waller (Bridge). Why? Because she's a British national treasure, it will boost tourism, and it will cost next to nothing (give or take a bit of signage), unlike Boris Johnson's 'Garden Bridge' across the River Thames, which cost £43 million and yet doesn't exist. While we're on the subject, Boris also blew £900,000 on a bridge between Scotland and Northern Ireland, and he spent years espousing the building of a new hub airport in the Thames Estuary called 'Boris Island' – neither of these exist either. It's almost like he spends his whole life talking out of his anal aperture. Oh, and let's not forget he has also called for a bridge to be built across the English Channel spanning the troubled waters between the UK and the continental Europe. This suggests he took policy advice from the twentieth-century Earth philosopher Simon and/or Garfunkel. If this is so, I suggest Mr Johnson leaves bridges alone forever more and instead opts for the sound of silence.

Hammersmith Bridge to be repaired, and renamed Wayne after the former England international footballer. He deserves it for putting up with John Terry.

Activists opposed to **High Speed Rail 2 (HS2) to be allowed to build their protest tunnel**, as long as it goes all the way to Birmingham; then they should build another one linking up Birmingham with Manchester.

1980s rocker Chris Rea to be installed as Britain's new

Transport Czar. Chris knows all about the problems on UK public transportation, with trenchant treatises such as *The Road to Hell* and *Driving Home for Christmas*. Indeed, his entire life has been devoted to inhabiting the middle of the road. His expertise can be ignored no longer. Bring him in. I know that he's getting on a bit, so I also espouse uploading his consciousness to the Cloud so that he can transcend corporeal existence and help humanity for as long as humanity lasts.

A hovercraft service to be reintroduced between Dover and Calais. But this time the crafts will actually hover. Human inventors merely talked a big game, but I'm a bin of my word.

Free parking between Vine Street and the Strand (for electric vehicles only).

Speaker phones to be banned on public transport. Offenders to be forced to watch the movie version of *Cats* every day for a year.

Segway use to be encouraged, on the basis that Segways are bigger, safer and sillier than e-scooters. To promote the benefits of this policy, in 2030 Formula 1 will be replaced by Segway racing: it's far more environmentally friendly, and who wouldn't want to see Lewis Hamilton and Max Verstappen duking it out around the famous streets of Monaco on a Segway? Maybe that's just me, but I doubt it.

One day every year, **escalators at train and tube stations are to be reversed**, encouraging travellers to go up the down escalators and down the up ones, as a free gym and *Gladiators* simulator all in one.

Anyone who chooses to use the stairs in between escalators

should be praised for doing so. Anyone who does so but has an insufferably smug look on their face while doing it must be punished through the medium of democracy: if all other passengers on the escalators press a button next to them at the same time, the staircase will transform into a slide and the self-satisfied git will be sent plummeting back to start the climb all over again.

A pedalo lane to be introduced on all rivers, canals and other inland waterways.

After Rishi Sunak had the nerve to pose for photographers at a petrol station filling up a Kia hatchback which he'd borrowed from a Sainsbury's employee to make him look more normal, **Rishi Sunak to be forced to fill up every hatchback in Britain** using his and his wife's massive personal fortune.

People who drive Range Rovers or Land Rovers in urban areas to be forced to take a replacement bus service once a week. Anyone caught as part of this scheme will have the right to ask for a more lenient punishment: namely euthanasia.

People who drive Mars Rovers or Lunar Rovers to appreciate intergalactic by-laws and realise that they can only park there during evenings or weekends. If they don't clear off, I'll have them clamped.

In my 2019 and 2021 manifestos, I broke the mould of transport politics by making the outlandish promise that I would finish Crossrail. Belatedly human politicians realised that this would be a good idea, and in celebration of the opening of the new Elizabeth Line, I propose that **the London Underground should be revamped by having all of its lines renamed**. So instead of the Bakerloo Line and the Victoria Line etc., there would be the following: Land, Guide, Punch, Head, Mascu, Bikini, Vase, Bread, Bee, Tan, Hot, Gaso, Help and of course Bin.*

Free bikes for everyone, to help combat obesity, traffic congestion and bike theft.

Amazon to be forced to introduce **a new and affordable method of public transport**, couriering people from A to B by drone. With guaranteed next-day delivery, this will be faster than many suburban rail services in Britain today.

On Heathrow expansion: Boris Johnson said that in order to stop a third runway he would lie in front of the bulldozers, which is the one good reason I can see for building it. Despite that, I would abandon plans for more UK runways in the future. Where we're going, we don't need runways.

A moratorium until 2030 on whether Birmingham should be converted into a star base.

The cruise industry to be reformed. Given the average age of cruise ship travellers, and the maxim that humans get more right wing as they get older, cruises are to be exclusively timed for UK general election periods. Meanwhile, the planet's oceans will be repopulated with icebergs, to help restrict climate change and cruise ship tourism all in one go.

---

* The odd human pedant (and I do mean odd) will point out that I have listed fourteen names but there are only eleven Underground lines. I'm well aware of that, so I'll also rename the Elizabeth Line, the Overground and the Docklands Light Railway. Or I'll build three new lines just to keep my word. Voters need to be able to trust their politicians.

The Treasury

In recent times, human stargazers have cottoned onto the fact that there might be a black hole at the centre of the Milky Way – an object named Sagittarius A*.* Well spotted, guys. It's not as if it has a mass equivalent to four million suns and it's been lying there for 100,000 years. But in their eagerness to look outwards into the/my cosmos, astronomers missed something even bigger. The most terrifying black hole in your solar system is Nefarious R, and it's sitting right under your noses in the United Kingdom's balance of payments. Decades of financial mismanagement by government after government have created a swirling vortex that poses a danger to all life as you know it. Someone needs to plug the hole, pronto.

Back home on Sigma IX, it's part of the job for any self-respecting politician to front up with the public and explain what their spending priorities are and how they are going to afford them. Seeing as my benevolent rule is totally unchallenged on my home world, I don't *have* to do this but hey, I'm nice like that. Earth's democrats seem to disagree. The only things on your planet that are certain are death, taxes and the sight of politicians being hideously vague about tax plans as they mooch around industrial sites in high-vis vests, trying to look like they've ever done a hard day's work.

---

* Originally called Sagittarius B, it has become yet another beneficiary of grade inflation. Incidentally, it amuses me that the reason you can tell this black hole resulted from the largest explosion ever to occur in your quadrant is because of the size of its circumnuclear disc, or CND.

The economic argument put forward by the 'mainstream' parties invariably amounts to gallons of drivel about how their policies are 'fully costed', without providing the slightest shred of evidence in support of their wild and baseless claims. This means that every human manifesto ever foisted onto voters has been worth less than a bog-standard roll of standard bog roll (it's a shame that hard copies of manifestos aren't more absorbent, or at least they'd be useful for something). Luckily I'm here to buck the trend. Because I'm not afraid to tell you precisely where I'll be getting the money from. And the paper this book is printed on is as officially as effective as Andrex supreme quilted triple ply. So whatever your views, you can rest easy that you haven't wasted your money.

A word of warning before we dive in, dear reader. Many humans think tax is dull, but you ignore it at your peril. A long time ago, in a galaxy quite close to mine, the taxation of trade routes to out-lying systems was in dispute, and after that things really kicked off.

My first key financial policy is to bring in more means testing, and lots of it. On Sigma IX, using sophisticated AI algorithms we are able to calibrate the amount each Recyclon should owe according to their income, wealth and assets, so everyone contrib-utes a fair share to public services without overly inconveniencing them. I notice that on Earth this simple idea is used only sparingly, and highly incompetently at that. Politicians (usually from the right wing) like to moan that thorough means testing is imprac-tical because it costs more money to implement than it makes in savings. Poppycock, I reply. OK, so the UK's testing capacity is far more primitive than mine, but I am happy to share with you a patented set of targeted criteria that will easily demarcate the haves from the have-nots. Follow these rules and you can't go wrong:

Do you currently send your children to private school?

Do you wear a cravat?

Have you ever referred to an evening meal as a 'kitchen supper'?

Did you spend most of 2020 in your charming weekend cottage in Padstow?

Is your surname Rees-Mogg?

If the answer to any of these questions is yes, you must pay higher rate tax on your income, assets and property (or more likely properties). If you answer yes to question five, you must pay double. After the pandemic, the UK treasury is estimated to have a £400 billion hole in it, but this simple questionnaire should go a long way to sorting it.

But that's just for starters. Here's a full list of my fiscal plans for the UK:

No croissant to be sold for more than £1. I've already mentioned this landmark progressive pledge, which swung thousands of votes my way in the 2021 London Mayoral Election. It's a no-brainer, and not in the UKIP sense of not having a brain. I hereby promise to roll out my flagship pastry initiative nationwide on day one of a Binface administration. While the evil spectre of excessive inflation cannot be stopped in its tracks by one single policy alone, this should put a decent dent into it.

A Hall of Shame for tax avoiders must be created. This will involve giant statues of Gary Barlow, Jimmy Carr, relevant cast members from *Mrs Brown's Boys* and other controversial figures being placed along the Mall in central London. Each one will be cast out of frozen faecal matter and have the word 'bastard' emblazoned on the pedestal.

The Chancellor's office to be fitted with a booster seat. When little Rishi was in Number 11, he couldn't even see his Excel spreadsheets. No wonder he didn't have a clue what was going on. Installing the booster seat post hoc will ensure that similar embarassment does not recur if the Treasury ends up being run by someone of similar stature to Mr Sunak, such as a house plant or child.

The Governor of the Bank of England to be chosen by lot, like jury service. Then the next year the role passes to whoever lives to the governor's immediate right, like the turns in a game of Monopoly. I'm aware of the fact that each banker will probably squirrel away some money from the bank for his/her own use during their time in control, but why change the habit of a lifetime? It will soon be academic because…

The Bank of England eventually to be made redundant, as the pound is harmonised with the Recyclo – my own currency – with a view to monetary union.

Billionaires who pay to travel into space to be taxed £1 billion per journey. Space is mine, so I'll charge this toll to any human tourist who breaches Earth's atmosphere and I'll plough the money into improving Britain (unless another country votes me into power first, in which case they can have the cash – that's democracy).

All existing tax havens in British overseas territories to

be abolished. In their place, one new haven is to be created, inside the Saxon Crown, a Wetherspoon's free house in Corby, Northamptonshire. If any rich human wishes to avoid tax, they will have to be domiciled there, and cameras will be installed inside the venue so that what happens in there on a daily basis can be sold as a brand new reality TV show with an exciting twist: no one can ever be voted out.

A new council tax band to be created. People who previously found themselves in bands A–C will now simply be in a new 'Banned' band, preventing them from having to pay the levy, with the super-rich making up the shortfall. How? By my most eye-catching Treasury policy of all…

Council Tax to be doubled for second homes. I will also triple it for third homes, quadruple it for fourth homes and so on (the royals won't like this). Redistribution gets no more satisfying, and this on its own should secure me multiple election victories in the future. To whichever journalist picks up on it first, cunningly buried here on page 175, you've got yourself a scoop.

A new 'Eat Out to Help Out' scheme to be introduced: all government ministers to be encouraged to eat out even more than they already do, to help civil servants try to clear up their latest mess without the idiots getting in the way.

Interest rates to be renamed because they don't interest people so much as bore them or strike terror into their hearts. They should instead be known as Clarkson rates, to be regulated by the independent Office of Banter Responsibility (OBR). At time of writing, the current Clarkson rate is 1.75 per cent – low, but still too high.

The furlough scheme to be reintroduced, for any photographer tasked with taking publicity shots of Liz Truss.

Further revenue-generating measures are outlined below in my plans for other departments. In the highly unlikely event that any extra money should be required to implement my manifesto, rest assured I'll just pinch some from the Oddurms on Sigma X when they're not looking. That should foot, and indeed fit, the bill. Those guys are scumbags and they deserve it.

PS. To anyone enquiring about my own tax status, I am happy to confirm that I am operating as a sole invader.

The Binistry of Defence

These are parlous times for planet Earth, when old certainties have crumbled and new wrinkles are scoring the botoxed face of post-war Europe. This places the United Kingdom in an awkward double bind – pressure is building for the nation's defence capability to be consolidated, just when the Treasury can least afford it. It's quite the pickle. How can this be solved? Simple. The answer lies with nuclear weapons. This subject is an old chestnut (if a chestnut could unleash armageddon) and one that traditionally splits the Labour Party along tribal lines – devoted peaceniks demand that Britain should unilaterally disarm, while their more centrist comrades believe that maintaining an independent deterrent is a safer position given the state of modern geopolitics. Never the twain shall meet, until now. My defence policy for the UK is unique in offering something that can appeal to everyone: I would make **a firm public commitment to go ahead with the £100 billion renewal of the Trident weapons system, followed by an equally firm private commitment not to go ahead with it**. They're secret submarines, so no one will ever know. It's a win-win. Stick the money in the NHS. Lovely stuff.

PS. I call this policy Nuke Zero.

PPS. We can't 100 per cent rule out the possibility that my proposal isn't in fact UK government policy already. I kinda hope that it is, but as the government and the armed forces can never own up to it, I'm extremely happy to own the idea for myself.

Having proved the reasonableness of my strategy – maximum threat, minimum damage – allow me to add the next key pillar of defence spending which must also be adopted by Britain forthwith. On 9 February 2022 it was reported on BBC News that a mysterious shortwave radio station called 'UVB-76', which is used by the Russian army for military communications, was hacked by a person or persons unknown and replaced with a signal that played a constant flow of Rick Astley's 'Never Gonna Give You Up'. To this day, nobody knows who did this. I'm saying nothing. All I'll say is that the weaponisation of 1980s power pop for battlefield use is something that is not outlawed by the Galacteva Convention (at least not yet) and I for one intend to take advantage of it. I suggest that the British Army does the same.

Of course having the right tools can only take you so far. A large part of military success on any planet comes down to morale. If your troops are truly up for the fight, they're going to be a lot more effective than if they've been conscripted and lied to by a mad nutjob. Pride is an invaluable possession to own and it can be surprisingly cheap to obtain. All it takes is some smart thinking. Thus I would harness the same power that was tapped into by the *Boaty McBoatface* phenomenon, and **offer soldiers the opportunity to name the Royal Navy's warships by public vote.** I humbly offer some suggestions to get the ball rolling:

HMS *M&S* (not just any warship)

HMS *PMS* (features terrifying strike capability)

HMS *DFS* (built to exploit short-term opportunities, especially on bank holiday weekends)

HMS *TMS* (an old ironclad which keeps going on and on, and surprisingly works better during rain)

HMS *DRS* (equipped with new technology to correct past errors and also reduce drag*)

HMS *VHS* (must be reversed before being returned to port)

HMS *SMS* (communications ship)

HMS *BHS* (out of commission)

HMS *SOS* (a phrase likely to be heard on board all of the above at some point)

My final defence policy is a simple one and should be adopted forthwith: **stop selling arms to Saudi Arabia; start buying lasers from Count Binface.**

---

* By which I mean the longitudinal retarding force upon the vessel, as opposed to cross-dressing. The latter I would never dream of outlawing in the Navy, for fear of mass desertions.

The Binistry Of Education

There is nothing more important than education. And not only in the ways of *Lovejoy* and Ceefax. Younglings are the future of the omniverse, and it's never been more important to prepare them for what adulthood on Earth will entail and to level with them about the complete pig's ear that their parents' generation has made of it all. Teaching unions can be a hard bunch to please, but I feel that I am on very comfortable ground discussing education reforms in the United Kingdom. Why? Have I been a teacher? No. Have I studied for a Postgraduate Certificate of Education (PGCE)? Nope. Have I any Earthly qualifications whatsoever that might hold me in good stead for the utterly vital task of schooling the nation's kids? Not a sausage. But on the other hand there is this unassailable fact: 'Sir' Gavin Williamson has held the post of UK Education Secretary, which means that literally anybody could do it.* And if they did, they would automatically be doing it better than at least one previous holder of the post.

In my bid to clean up Gav's mess, I'm keen to help as many younglings as I can. And here's how:

No matter what solar system you call home, it's crazy how tiny the margin can sometimes be between success and failure at school. The key to doing well is motivation. Let me give you a little example. If you bunk off from lessons on Friday afternoon for no reason, you could find yourself behind in your studies and on the fast track to a harder life. But if you bunk off on Friday afternoons

---

* Aim high, kids. *Anything* is possible.

and call it a climate change protest, you could be on the express lane to global celebrity and a Nobel Prize. Having purpose is the key. And an advanced knowledge of modern public relations doesn't hurt either. This is why all younglings on Sigma IX now receive **thirty hours of free media training from reception year onwards,** and I would encourage that this should be adopted on Earth too. There is little point in nurturing your little Johnny or Jenny to become a highly successful adult if they can be undone by a compromising drunken tweet they sent in their teenage years. It's a jungle out there, people. Let me be your Tarzan.

On Sigma IX, all binlings are given a choice on how to be assessed for their qualifications: exam or algorithm. The algorithm probes the deepest crevices of each child's mind to discover precisely how much they've learned about the subject, whereas the exam tests their ability to cram a select amount of facts through tears of stress the night before. 100 per cent of pupils choose the exam. We allow a coursework element too, but only a small one. We're not naive. I would offer this system to kids on Earth on a voluntary basis.

On university tuition fees: these should be charged to any politician or canvasser who has ever campaigned for them, payable every year for the rest of their life in line with inflation. Any shortfall in funding the tertiary sector is to be made up by charging Nick Clegg the full remaining amount from his juicy Meta pay packet.

Starting age for kids at primary school: in the UK this currently stands at four years old, which is relatively early. I suggest that before they become inculcated in classroom learning, first they should be given the chance to do something more age-appropriate, such as writing opinion columns for the *Daily Telegraph*, presenting a show on GB News, and negotiating post-Brexit trade deals.

On secondary schools: for decades there has been debate across the UK about the merits of selective and comprehensive education, and I am led to believe that modern thinking leans away from the creation of new grammar schools. I am happy to take this human expertise on board, and instead my flagship reform will bring in a new wave of Gamma Schools, founded on three key principles: one, better pay for teachers to attract bright graduates; two, increased facilities, including more playing fields; and three, any child caught misbehaving three times will be blasted into deep space, with the parents being offered a lovely fruit basket by way of consolation or celebration, depending on the child. Discipline is a key issue in schools, but that should do the trick.

On private schools: I'm quite new around here so I might be wrong, but from what I can glean, twenty-first-century education in Britain might just have an imbalance between the state and independent sectors. I say imbalance. I mean chasm. This is strange to me because we don't have such segregation on Sigma IX. All Binlings go to the same kind of schools so that they all get a fair start in life. Is that crazy? Maybe it is.

When it comes to the independent sector, Eton, Harrow, Winchester and the like will be banned from being called 'public' schools for a start, because that's just taking the piss. Even an alien can tell from a glance that they're *private* schools, and there's no point hiding it. I will also strip them of their charity status on day one of a Binface government. On other planets, charities are non-profit organisations working for the benefit of needy sections of society, not exclusive entities that entrench privilege and success among the establishment, poisoning social mobility in the process. I've got a sneaky feeling that for decade after decade, private schools have been getting away with a cheeky tax giveaway from the government, and it's high time that this was zapped into oblivion.

As for the sheer existence of private education, I don't subscribe to the views of some human lefties who think the whole thing should be abolished forthwith. That's a bit *Citizen Smith* for my tastes.* And it would never be accepted by the British establishment, because it would directly affect the schooling of their little Henrys and Henriettas. So instead I have a moderate, sensible solution: **the abolition of all UK private schools will take place on Friday 1 January in the year 2100**. That way, nobody alive today will be affected but the overall education standards of future generations will be vastly improved. Take that, Bojo the clown and all your mates. This is what I call levelling up.

Until the year 2100 is reached, there is space for the UK to adopt a more moderate reforming measure. Under my plans, former students of Eton College will be banned from becoming Prime Minister for at least such time as it takes for there to have been more women to hold the post than ex-pupils of that school.

---

* I don't just watch *Lovejoy*, you know. Indeed, from my understanding of Earthian culture, I would suggest that Citizen Smith is the *Citizen Kane* of artworks that begin with 'Citizen'. Power to the People (human and non-human)!

The current score is Etonians 20, Women 3, so this should keep the top hat brigade out of Number 10 for a while.

The Binistry of the Environment

If there is any area of policy that requires urgent attention it is surely this one. Your planet is slow-cooking its way to annihilation, and you humans are the ones who switched on the oven without reading the instructions. It's not too late to sort things out but, my word, you're cutting it fine. And just because the recent drama-documentary *Don't Look Up* accurately predicted the arrival of the next asteroid doesn't mean that you should stop caring about the time that your planet has left. I relish the opportunity to propose some greener, cleaner solutions to Britain's creaking infrastructure, while cutting through the bovine faecal matter that pollutes debate on your planet. Take this statement reported by Sky News in 2019, that 'Heathrow has become carbon neutral in emissions, but only from the parts of the airport that it runs and not including flights.' If you ask me, their press office could do with reducing their emissions for a start.

What can be done to halt the crisis? Behold my planet-saving suite of environmental policies to save Britain and Earth:

Piers Morgan to be zero emissions by 2030. Certain independent bodies have suggested that a 2050 target is more achievable, but I honestly think that if everyone pulled together in a sort of wartime effort, it could be done. At the time of writing, we've got the best part of a decade to make Piers not on the TV, radio or internet. And things are going well. With ratings as low as

10,000 viewers for his TalkTV show 'Uncensored'*, Piers is doing his bit to help make this dream a reality. #YesWeCan.

A massive expansion in recycling in all sectors, except Hollywood movie plots.

Single-use plastic to be phased out entirely. This means that the next series of *Love Island* should only feature contestants from previous series. It should also be set on a remote island, last for ten years, and to save power it shouldn't be televised. But the contestants shouldn't be told about that final detail. Put together, this might sound like sentencing a bunch of annoying young people to a life of punishing exile. Because that's what it is.

I note that there is increasing interest in the idea of **'rewilding'** – which involves reintroducing wolves to the UK and allowing them to roam the countryside. I like this idea but it could be dangerous for humans, so I would license a pilot scheme whereby the wolves are released at a test location, on Jeremy Clarkson's farm, to see how the two species get on (the wolves should be given the scent of diesel, Old Spice and cholesterol to set them on the right track).

On a similar note, I am in favour of **the legalisation of the hunting of fox-hunters**.

I propose **knocking down the Millennium Dome** and replacing it with a nature reserve, giving humans and animals a place in London by the river where they can enjoy the fresh air. It will be called the O2.

---

* If a ranting tree falls in a forest and nobody is there to hear it, does it matter if it's censored?

London Fields should be improved, specifically by the provision of new public toilet facilities, which must all be signposted 'WC Fields'.

I note that the Prince of Wales/King Charles[*] has taken an unusual step to help conserve the environment, by converting his Aston Martin to run on surplus English white wine (which coincidentally tastes of petrol), in combination with the whey from cheese. This is an ingenious solution from His Royal Highness which, if it can be rolled out across the nation, could enable all of **Britain's cars to be fuelled by the leftovers from parties at 10 Downing Street**.

At Trafalgar Square, David Attenborough should be put on the fourth plinth, or a statue of him. Either's fine by me.

'Bags for Life': This is a well-intentioned initiative but a 10p charge per bag is far too small a deterrent to stop shoppers from always buying a new bag with their groceries – or, more likely, taking one without paying. To deal with miscreants I would ensure that judges are empowered in sentencing: very simply, people who have such a bag but don't use it should get life. And indeed a life.

Renewable power: I am strongly in favour of the increased use of wind, a resource in which British politics is very well resourced. However, I'm more interested in deeds than words and so I would dispense with any of Boris Johnson's vapid old sloganeering about turning the UK into 'the Saudi Arabia of wind'. A good government should of course aspire to being the

---

[*] Just doing a spot of future-proofing.

Saudi Arabia of nothing whatsoever, and in this instance Bojo's bullshit is particularly unfortunate in its connotations, given the sharpness of windmill blades and the likelihood of them making contact with citizens' hands or necks. To help meet demand, I shall sell the government a set of patented Count Binface windmills, which will be (laser-armed and) entirely safe. But wind can only ever be part of the solution. When it comes to solving the UK's future energy mix, the best thing that any civilisation can do is to create power from whatever you have a surplus of: on Sigma IX, that is starlight, water and hydrogen. On Earth, it's hot air, princes, plastic, imitation KFC restaurants, non-imitation KFC restaurants, and lies. Harness those and you'll never need another drop of dodgy oil.

Whatever the fuel, when it comes to building new power stations you have to brace yourself for **the NIMBU element**: the grumpy minority who oppose any attempts at development in their area and scream, 'Not in my bloody universe!' A wise government listens to all arguments and is sensitive to environmental concerns, taking care not to disturb the green asteroid belt but always on the lookout for promising opportunities. Back home, I've turned the entirety of one of my moons – Meganon – into a giant fusion reactor, which has powered planet Sigma IX for centuries with cheap and clean energy. As a by-product it has meant that on another of my moons – Mikron – the view out of residents' conservatories has been totally ruined. But hey, sometimes you just gotta build.

Dear Greta

Before we leave the subject of the environment, I would like to take the opportunity to send a message to Greta Thunberg – the mighty Earth activist who I think is as cool as she'd like the oceans to be, and who in recent times has gone a bit rogue, with her choice of fruity language to condemn human politicians. A bit like Kylie's grunge period, you might say. Greta is keen to stay at the cutting edge of scientific and political developments so I assume she's reading this. So allow me to address her directly: Gretz, mate, let's have an interplanetary summit. I know that sometimes you've been single-handedly fighting the forces of right-wing, reactionary politicians and that you possess an amazing ability to get their backs up. Well fear not, because I'm here to give you back-up in getting their backs up. We are the coalition that nobody's expecting, but which everybody needs. If Robbie Williams and Nicole Kidman can be a hit combo, we can do it too.

The Binistry of (Poetic) Justice

The twenty-first Earth century is proving to be a time when, more than ever, there is a small tranche of society whose attitude to the rules can be summed up by the three Bs – bending, breaking and burning them. These people are known collectively by another B – 'bastards' – and come the glorious day they will be brought to book by yet another B – the Binistry of Poetic Justice. This department will be dedicated to dispensing some much-needed karma, giving the fat cats of Britain and beyond who need it a good kicking.*

Housing

The provision of affordable homes is a *perennial political problem*, something which is just as hard to fix as it is to say quickly five times in a row. But I believe I can offer a solution. **I would demand that the estates of controversial magnates such as Sir Philip Green are turned into land for social housing**. Now it's fair to say that among the wealthy elite of British society this policy would kick up more than a bit of a stink, but I've anticipated their opposition and I have an answer for that too. Using patented Count Binface cloaking technology, the newly created high-rise blocks that I propose to build will be completely hidden from sight, preserving the rural landscape and meaning that Mr Green need never know that we've nicked all his land. Instead all he will see is a sudden influx of ramblers who keep appearing and disappearing through invisible doors, and he will become so confused that he'll go mad. With any luck.

Meanwhile, alongside my policy of turning all spare royal palaces into shelters for the homeless (it shouldn't take a talking bin to say that homelessness needs to be disposed of), I will also **requisition every property belonging to Russian oligarchs and hand them free of charge to Ukrainian refugees**. I would say that you'd have to be heartless to disagree with this, but seeing

---

* I'm speaking proverbially here. I'm not some kind of extraterrestrial Kurt Zouma.

as Michael Gove supports the idea, it seems even the sans-heart are on board for this one, which is great news.

The Phantom Zone

The Phantom Zone is a realm of space where criminals from across the galaxy, as well as people I just don't like – let's call them baddies – can be safely ensconced and not cause anyone any harm any more. It is a long-standing pledge of mine to banish a targeted group of such baddies into exile. Since I started keeping a tally in 2017, the roster of individuals from Earth who deserve an eternal stay in the ol' PZ has been growing all the time, but top of my list of ne'er-do-wells right now are the following: Piers Corbyn, Michael Gove, Katie Hopkins, Donald Trump, Rupert Murdoch, Matt Hancock, Nick Clegg, Vladimir Putin, Sergei Lavrov and Bono. The best thing of all about this policy is that it comes with the added bonus of a ready-to-go primetime TV entertainment format, in which viewers get to decide who, from a shortlist of offenders, should be expelled to the P-Zone.

Incidentally, if you're interested in learning more about the Phantom Zone, an excellent Earth-based filmmaker named Richard Donner produced a highly informative documentary about it called *Superman II*. It's worth checking out.

Drugs

Being a progressive bin, I am keen to revolutionise drugs policy in the UK and so I am happy to match Sadiq Khan's 2021 promise to **establish an independent commission that will examine the decriminalisation of cannabis.** But I will go further and ensure that this commission is always well stocked with snacks, to maintain concentration among the munchies-addled contributors. I also want to focus attention on the bigger problem of the amount of Class A drugs that are sloshing around Britain. Believe it or not, in London this has caused the eels that live in the River Thames to get hooked on cocaine, so much so that the eels have become really annoying and won't stop talking about themselves. It needs sorting out. However, I will focus even more of my energies on the biggest problem of all, which is the massive asteroid that is still hurtling towards Earth, and which is going to leave everyone – and I do mean everyone – very much stoned.

The Terrestrial Office

Always a tricky one for humans, this, balancing law and order with civil rights. But that's because of who you tend to put in charge. If you will have the likes of Priti Patel running the shop, for three minutes let alone three years, you're going to end up with a shop that's on fire. Fortunately my policies have the power to douse her crazy flames:

When it comes to the Police, there's a lot of rubbish that seems to float around them. Especially 'De Do Do Do, De Da Da Da'. What a load of nonsense that was. I pledge to cut through the crap, and outdo-do-do the Tories, by **investing in 20,001 more police officers.**

Having got the cops on side with this new recruitment drive, next

I will encourage the new Metropolitan Police Commissioner Mark Rowley to move on from the old regime of Cressida Dick by taking the unprecedented step of announcing that it is part of the police's job to investigate crimes that took place in the past.

I will reinstate citizens' right to peaceful protest, while also protecting public order. Other nations on Earth are taking intriguing steps in this regard. In February 2022, for instance, authorities in New Zealand took the unusual step of playing on loudspeakers a fifteen-minute loop of Barry Manilow's greatest hits, plus the 'Macarena', as a means of dislodging demonstrators who had been camped outside the country's parliament building. I promise never to do such a thing, and only ever to control riots with my patented range of Count Binface lasers, which are substantially more humane than a round of Barry.

The Northern Ireland Protocol: I would amend this so that any Czechs on the Irish border are allowed to stay there. What have they done wrong? Nothing. Leave them to it.

Jacob Rees-Mogg to be prorogued.

Most importantly of all, as we've covered earlier in the book, **the hand-dryer at the Crown & Treaty, Uxbridge must be moved to a more sensible position**. Any politician serious about preventing civil unrest knows that this is non-negotiable. However, if you're worried that my passion for sanely placed hand-drying machines stops in Uxbridge (and South Ruislip), have no fear! I shall campaign for a nationwide common-sense adjustment of all such offending machines, including a similar atrocity at the Crown & Greyhound, Dulwich (as pointed out to me by a follower on Twitter). Is it a mere coincidence that these dysfunctional institutions appear to be linked to the Crown? Probably, but you never know.

The Binistry of Digital, Culture, Media and Ceefax

Whatever your species, whether Recyclon, human or Raab, we all live in an information age. The provision of culture and safeguarding truth are the kind of ideas which you'd think any civilised society should be able to take for granted, but on your planet it seems this isn't so. As a result this will be one of the most important Binistries of all, which will be given a broad sphere of influence and tasked with ~~controlling~~ taking care of all aspects of the media, to create a digital landscape that benefits ~~me~~ Earthlings.

We must begin with one of my most eye-catching policies of all: **the nationalisation of Adele**. Let's face it, she's just too damn good. Just think of what could be achieved if she was taken into public ownership. Huge multinationals are already buying up the back catalogues of great singers like Bruce Springsteen and Sting, and singers like Bob Dylan. Purchasing the artists themselves is the next logical step, and I want the UK to be at the forefront of this exciting new market. Adele on her own would be a powerful addition to the nation's economic might, but I see no reason to stop there, and in phase two I would nationalise Ed Sheeran, Stormzy and all Radiohead albums with the possible exception of *Hail to the Thief*. This revolutionary policy will need careful oversight and I have the perfect minion in mind to manage this process – Chris Rea. I know I've already given him the transport brief, which would keep a mainstream politician busy for decades, but I'm confident that Chris (or his uploaded virtual consciousness) will have sorted the roads and rail within a fortnight, so this will give him something else juicy to get stuck into.

On the subject of cultural spending, I will ensure that a pot of public money is diverted into music research, and specifically into Coldplay – to examine how that was allowed to happen. I need to know, because from an alien's standpoint it just doesn't make any sense. To show you that I take such matters seriously, I have already conducted a highly scientific poll on Twitter, in which I asked the very question, 'How do you explain Coldplay?' Here are the results:

- Jumped species:	9 per cent
- Lab leak:	18 per cent
- Deliberate bio-weapon:	73 per cent

Shocking, but not surprising. Still, at the time of writing, a great deal more research needs to be conducted into this issue, and a great deal of care will need to be given to those who conduct the research.

Ross Kemp to be the next Poet Laureate.

Modern art: speaking as a giant receptacle of waste material, I love the Turner Prize, and I would do absolutely nothing to change it. Sterling work, guys. Keep it up.

Modern books: as I see it, the fate of the Booker Prize is more open to debate, and will rest on how the critics (and Richard and Judy) take to this book. I suggest they take to it well.

Following on from Adele's success in getting the streaming platform Spotify to remove the shuffle button from her albums, **Mumford and Sons should have the play button removed** from theirs.

Classic FM should be folded into the social care system, being as it is the place where TV newsreaders go to die. Sir Trevor McDonald, John Suchet, Moira Stuart, John Humphrys, Nicholas Owen – they're all residents at the only care home in the world that broadcasts on DAB, smart speaker and 100–102 FM.

Decisions over whether controversial statues should remain in public places should be taken by local democratic vote. The exception to this is the number of wonderful, sacred temples that humans have dedicated to me and which are getting bigger all the time. You call them 'landfills' and I call them 'fanzones', and I thank you for them.

In future, 'God Save the King' should be replaced by a new national anthem: 'Never Gonna Give You Up' by Rick Astley – both because it's a stonking tune, and to ensure that Charles gets Rickrolled at every opportunity.

I will abolish hunger. You might think that's a strange pledge to include in my culture policies, but it will make sense when I point out that this will extinguish the need for the kind of charity campaign that enabled 'LadBaby' to curl out four successive Christmas number ones (each one being a bona fide musical number two), usurping a hard-won record of three in a row that was previously shared by the Beatles and the Spice Girls. The lack of global hunger anywhere on Earth would be an additional benefit.

To save younglings from the embarrassment of admitting to the first album they ever owned, **whenever parents register an Earth child's birth, they will be legally obliged to buy for their newborn not only a birth certificate but also a copy of** *Now That's What I Call Music 7*, so that everyone starts on a level playground. Specifically a Level 42 playground.

On podcasting: I have heard it said that a 'podcast' is the collective noun for a group of white men who talk too much. It's also a type of radio programme, which has mushroomed into a pandemic even more transmissible than SARS-CoV-2, with no known vaccine – although spread can be minimised by the use of earplugs. There was a time when podcasting was an egalitarian opportunity which allowed ordinary people to create successful programmes, but I note that more recently the market has been flooded with celebrities looking to get in on the act. I see a clear opportunity here to rebalance the landscape and make a few quid in the process: every podcast must be taxed at a rate of 10 per cent per stand-up comedian who appears on it. On the other hand, I pledge to offer generous tax credits for any humans who don't have a podcast of their own. (This ingenious policy has the twin benefits of being highly popular and very cheap.) Earthlings may be relieved to hear that your rash of podcasting is a phenomenon that's not exclusive to Earth: we have experienced similar outbreaks on Sigma IX, where the biggest hit show is a long-running series called 'My Dad Hasn't Made a Podcast'. They fill arenas with this stuff, as Recyclon listeners can't get enough of it. Thanks to sensible taxation, my Exchequer takes home a slice of the pie.

Count Binface to be the UK's entry at the Eurovision Song Contest every year for the next fifty years. *The Masked Singer* has proved the public have an appetite for exotic, oversized vocalists, so let's weaponise the idea to conquer Europe. Sam Ryder reached second place with a song about space. To go one step better, the UK needs to harness a singer *from* space. Unleash the Bin for the win!

Gladiators **to be reinstated** for the Saturday primetime schedules, but with a crucial difference from previous piss-poor attempts at a reboot: this new season must feature the original gladiators from series one, up against age-appropriate contenders. It'll knock *Squid Game* into a cocked Atlasphere. And humans will love me for it.

One of the biggest threats to the fabric of democracy on planet Earth is the proliferation of Fake News. It's for this reason that in my time as a politician on your world I have consistently turned down interview requests from controversial outlets that do nothing but spray a torrent of unrelenting bullshit, such as RT (formerly Russia Today), George Galloway's radio show on Sputnik FM (nope, I've never heard of it either) and *The One Show*. **I will ban all of these from being broadcast,** obviously, but by way of compensation, I will allow RT to be nominated for a Best Original Screenplay award at the BAFTAs for their commitment to fictional storytelling.

On sport: I am a big fan of Earth sports, especially basketball and netball, which involve putting something inside something else, and also curling, which features lots of sweeping. Maybe it's my Binnish heritage speaking but I find those activities all very satisfying. Being intimately connected with rubbish as I am, I'm also an avid follower of the England men's Test cricket team, even when they win. But clearly planet Earth's number one sport is football, and I can see why – it's brilliant. In fact, so excited am I by this simple game (and its potential for multi-billion-credit income) that I have exported it to outer space. Thanks to me, football is now a big hit on billions of alien worlds (the only places not to fall for its charms are the ones that don't have any gravity to speak of, which can be a bit of a problem). As a result, I am pleased to give readers of this book the exclusive news that the planet Lettibu in my quadrant is mounting an audacious bid to host the 2034 FIFA World Cup. Summer temperatures there can reach 140°C, several thousand Lettibunese workers have died while building the stadia, and the government has bribed FIFA with over a trillion dollars of kickbacks. So they're surely in with a shout of winning the bid.

As for how I would manage 'the beautiful game' on Earth, **I'd slap every club who tried to create a breakaway European Super League with an immediate relegation to non-league status** in their country: if they don't want to be part of the football pyramid, their wish is my command. I would also **bin the proposal of holding a World Cup every two years** and, for coming up with such a silly idea, I shall banish Arsene Wenger to a spell in the Phantom Zone (he should be fine with this, because I understand that from his time as Arsenal manager he's no stranger to sendings off). Meanwhile **the 'Fit and Proper Persons Test', which judges**

whether someone is appropriate or not to own a professional club, will be somewhat expanded so that obvious oligarchs and repressive Middle Eastern regimes are moved from the 'fit' column to the 'totally and obviously unfit' column. Finally, to cap his wonderful career, **I will present Tottenham and England striker Harry Kane with the trophy he so desperately craves.** It will be the 'Best Player Never To Win a Trophy' Trophy, which unfortunately, given the nature of it, I'll have to take back as soon as he's won it. But it's the least that Mr Kane deserves.

The BBC

For readers picking up this book after the year 2025, the BBC was a publicly funded broadcasting corporation with a precious global reputation until it was attacked and destroyed by extreme forces in the UK and abroad. **I will bring back and reboot the Beeb**, adding an extra B for Binface to make it the BBBC. I'm emboldened to tackle the thorny issue of this cherished broadcaster in the wake of Nadine Dorries having risen to become the UK's Culture Secretary. Previously I'd assumed that this position would require a sophisticated understanding of the media landscape, but it turns out that being a novice who belongs on another planet is no impediment.

For the important role of BBBC Director General I would be happy to take the reins myself, but if I'm a bit busy running the omniverse, then I have in mind just the pair of humans to turn Auntie's fortunes around: first I would turn to John Craven, because the Craven One is unanimously loved and he understands that, like your planet, the news is round. And I love his jumpers too. He's a unifying force and that's something your planet desperately needs. Joining John in a job share of running the BBBC will be the unimpeachably wonderful Baroness Floella Benjamin. Once I abolish the Lords she'll be at a loose end, and she's far too brilliant not to be working in public service. What's more, with Britain's human politicians treating the media like a pack of unruly children with a toy box, Floella has the ideal credentials to keep the little brats in check. When it comes to wider reforms of the corporation, John and Flo will be delighted to know that I've already done a lot of the heavy lifting myself, and I hereby present a set of measures that should be implemented immediately, for the benefit of all species:

Let's get the obvious one out of the way first. **Ian McShane to be offered a blank cheque to bring back TV masterpiece** *Lovejoy* with a new six-thousand-part series. The box set will be taught as part of the national curriculum.

The commentator for all major constitutional events including royal weddings and the state opening of Parliament must be Craig Charles.

Craig Charles also to be reinstated as presenter of a new series of *Robot Wars* on primetime BBC One, and for his services to motorised mayhem he is to be knighted. If Sir Killalot can have one, Craig certainly should. I must add that this is all on the proviso that I can enter my robot, Mecha-Pasquale, into the competition. It's equipped with ultra-high-pitched sonic weaponry to disintegrate opponents' armour and shatter their operators' eardrums (I've got a sneaky feeling I might win).

***Strictly Come Dancing* must strive towards a greater display of diversity.** Sure, they have broken the television mould multiple times by featuring same-sex couples, Paralympians and a deaf celebrity (the peerless Rose), but where are the aliens? Would I accept an invitation from Strictly? I'd revel in it. Actually, I'd Revel-Horwood in it, darlings. The entire omniverse is crying out to see me and Nancy perform our American smooth, and to watch Craig get plasma-zapped if he dares utter a word of criticism about my pivots while in hold (my laser aim is fab-u-lous).

Incidentally, while we're on the subject of *Strictly*, I must just take a moment to thank Dave Arch and his wonderful band.

As a matter of urgency, **Children In Need should really get round to fixing Pudsey's eye.** The BBC's official charity has been running since 1980 but they still haven't sent their lead presenter to a decent ophthalmologist, and you'd be forgiven for thinking that the whole thing is a massive hoax. Conspiracy theories have certainly started from less. 'Have you actually seen Great Ormond Street Hospital? It's crawling with lizards.' It's only a matter of time before this kind of claptrap becomes the 5G loonies' next bandwagon. So come on people, get Pudsey sorted. And if he needs some laser treatment done on the cheap, give me a call.

Saturday afternoon extravaganza *Grandstand* to be brought back immediately, no matter what sports the corporation is able to afford to show. In fact, the more obscure the activity the better, to my mind. What could be better than whiling away a weekend watching the World Rubik's Cube Championship or an upgraded, crazy golf version of the Ryder Cup? I'm also very happy to discuss licensing the rights to Sigma IX's favourite sport, 3D snooker.

The Archers **should be stopped for a year, just to see what happens.** Shorn of the planet's longest-running drama, would agricultural productivity go up? It certainly can't hurt to try. All actors will be compensated, and indeed promoted, with regular guest roles on *Doctors*.

What on Earth? With Count Binface, my 2021 radio special featuring exclusive interviews with former MPs Martin Bell and Heidi Allen, which incidentally is available to listen to right now on BBC Sounds, **must be heavily promoted on the front page of the BBC News website for eternity**. It's public service broadcasting at its finest.

I mentioned in my Treasury policies that only three things on Earth are certain: death, taxes and the sight of politicians in high-vis vests. But on your planet there is in fact a fourth inescapable fact of life: Jools Holland's annual hootenanny. This is the most frightening of the lot, and as a result humans will be delighted to know that I have succeeded in developing a vaccine against it. It is called the 'mute button' and in this instance a single jab will suffice (take that, Pfizer and Moderna). To help eradicate the problem **I'm launching a range of omniversal remote controls at cost price.** Once this preventative measure is fully rolled out I shall turn my attention to finding efficacious treatments that can relieve symptoms for the many millions of people who continue to suffer from the debilitating effects of Long Jools.

This leaves the question of how the corporation should handle its New Year's Eve coverage. I believe I can offer a fresh perspective because we have an entirely different approach on Sigma IX. It's a particularly acute issue because our planet has two suns as opposed to your measly one, which means we get to celebrate New Year's Eve twice a year. And what we do is very simple: we hold a big musical jamboree featuring a host of stars from across the stars, but our ones actually take place on New Year's Eve, as opposed to the BBC's BIG LIE, and ours have the crucial distinction of lacking Jools Holland, which makes all the difference. (Weirdly, even on our Sigma IX version, Ruby Turner and Suggs seem to turn up every time, but some things are out of even my control.) As for what to do with Jools himself, I can think of no better background music for the Phantom Zone than a never-ending torrent of boogie-woogie piano, so I'll be packing him off there. #MUTENANNY.

As you will have read from my above proposals, the BBBC will have to think very carefully before it cancels any of its much-loved formats, because more often than not their supposed cost-cutting measures cause more harm than good. Take the fabled science magazine show *Tomorrow's World*, for instance. Corporation bosses cancelled it just before the series was about to air an episode forecasting the gallons of shit that was to rain down upon TV Centre and Broadcasting House in the decades to come. It's a shame, because otherwise they might have been able to forestall crises such as QueenGate, Martin Bashir, faked competitions, Jonathan Ross and Russell Brand's Sachsgate furore, the ageism dispute brought by Miriam O'Reilly, the gender pay dispute raised by Carrie Gracie, the continued employment and posthumous veneration of Jimmy Savile, and most egregious of all, multiple series commissions of *Mrs Brown's Boys*. Not that the precious Beeb has been mismanaged over the last forty years or anything. If only they'd kept this prophetic televisual beacon alive, all of the palaver could have been avoided, thanks to those modern day Cassandras, Howard Stableford, Maggie Philbin and Judith Hann. What's more, Kieran Prendiville would be able to apologise to viewers for claiming on national television that compact discs were indestructible (nobody's perfect).

Ceefax

Why do I take such an interest in the venerable British Broadcasting Corporation? One word says it all: Ceefax. Any organisation with the vision and audacity to have dreamed up the omniverse's finest creation deserves saving, no matter how many times their senior management has trodden in a Mrs Brown. Long-standing followers of mine will know that while all my manifesto points are absolute bangers, standing head and shoulders above everything else is my flagship policy: Ceefax must be restored immediately, with all Teletext services including the Oracle and Bamboozle being rolled out within the first hundred days of my first government.

If you're not familiar with the word Ceefax, firstly congratulations on being so young, and secondly I should explain that it is an ingenious (and supposedly obsolete) service that was born on 23 September 1974 and involved electronic news and information being transmitted within analogue television signals, appearing on your home TV in a mixture of colourful text and blocky graphics. The result was a kind of primitive website, and what it lacked in speed it more than made up for in being unhackable by Russians, impervious to trolls, and a portal to affordable holidays. Even better, it was often broadcast late at night, accompanied by a lovely soundtrack of lilting dinner jazz. What's not to like? It is *Homo sapiens'* greatest contribution to the omniverse, and I applaud you for it.

I am delighted to see that since I put Ceefax back on the agenda, it has trended on Twitter and a young human in Belfast named Nathan Dane has even created his own amateur Teletext emulator, proving that this dream is within humanity's compass. But my interest in it is not only aesthetic. Planet Earth has never more needed the help of a friendly, colourful and sober news service that's free from sidebars, pop-ups, cookies and crap. And that's because you need an antidote to the internet.

The year 1989 was when the crisis started, because that was the moment when Tim Berners-Lee, that supervillain in a dicky-bow, invented the World Wide Web. As he did so, he famously declared, 'This is for everyone,' which sounds like a peerless act of altruism but might actually have been the cackling threat of a demented maniac (allegedly). You don't need me to tell you how things have been going since then. In the blink of an optical organ, your planet has gone round the bend as it has desperately wrestled with the effects of this new technology. If an alien like me wreaked such havoc on your species, you'd fairly accuse me of trying to destroy you. But far from being punished, Tim was knighted – for his services to pornography, I assume.

There's a simple reason why humans have had their lives turned upside down by the internet, which is that you went and did things in the wrong order. I'm very fond of a civilisation called the Delonauts, whose first hundred years as an internet-enabled species ushered in a period of peace, decorum and gentility that humans should envy. It was the Delonauts' Golden Age, a time free from trolling, name-calling, hate-spreading and GIFs. How did they achieve this utopian state? By the act of creating their World Wide Web a full Delo-century before any citizen was legally allowed to invent a computer with which to access it. This was a shrewd plan that gave the Delonauts plenty of time for the concept of the Web to bed in, so that everyone would be ready to use it responsibly when the time came. On Launch Day there were street parties all over the planet, as citizens celebrated being able to build and buy machines that could get online. Within a week, the entire population had gone mad. But you've got to admire their thought process. And it's still arguably preferable to what's happening on Earth right now.

But it's not too late for the United Kingdom. Choose Life. Choose Ceefax.

The Binistry of Health

Last but not least in my policy bonanza, we must consider the biggest fish of all:[*] the National Health Service. It's an astonishing achievement and the envy of the galaxy. Never has there been

---

* Give or take Ceefax.

a single institution that's done more to support life, and never more than in the early 2020s has there been a government that's done more to put it on life support. In case the Tories get their way and you're reading this after 2025, by the way, the NHS was a much-loved healthcare system that was free at the point of use until every last inch of flesh was ripped off it by a succession of greedy ministers and fat-cat privateers. Fortunately, at the time that I'm writing this at least, in 2022, reports of its death are exaggerated. What's more, a vote for Count Binface will ensure that the NHS both survives and thrives, with my pledge to invest a modest £1 trillion a week into the health system.

Apart from money, though, is there anything else that can be done to help fix the dear old NHS? Indeed there is. I have these further suggestions.

Mask wearing should be encouraged, not only during pandemics. They help to stop the spread of infectious diseases, and according to a study by researchers at Earth's Cardiff University, they make people look more attractive too.*

Any politician who claims they're building forty new hospitals when they're actually repurposing old ones should be imprisoned for forty years.†

Anyone called Dido Harding should be banned from working in or near the NHS.

---

* The study was published in the journal *Cognitive Research: Principles and Implication*, which is available at no good newsagents. But they clearly know a thing or two about attractiveness.

† The government of Boris Johnson enjoyed varying their number of imaginary hospitals, from 40 to 42 to even 48. So just to be sure to cover it, all former Conservative Health Secretaries should be sentenced to 480 years in jail.

Anyone who has ever employed Dido Harding should be banned from working in or near planet Earth.

Any (former) Health Secretary who has shares in their sister's company, which just happened to win lucrative NHS contracts during the pandemic, should be sent straight to the Phantom Zone.

If another pandemic comes along and causes your planet once again to be plagued by plague (spoiler alert: it will), access to vaccines will be paramount. Human scientists will have taken great heart from their anti-Covid jabs that they can create new vaccines from scratch at a quicker rate than was previously thought possible. (Bravo to everyone on that.) But I am certain that there could be improvements in the delivery of jabs into arms, in terms of both speed and accuracy. Therefore during the next global health emergency **I will conscript the world's finest professional darts players to lead the vaccination effort**. Who are the most qualified people on the planet to deliver finely targeted shots? It's Phil 'The Power' Taylor. It's Dave 'Chissy' Chisnall. It's Peter 'Snakebite' Wright. Get them in! You could televise it and it would make millions. It would pay for itself. Another Binface policy, another win-win. (While they're at it, the dartists could surreptitiously vaccinate a good few anti-vaxxers along the way. They'd never know they'd been jabbed, and in this unique instance, what they don't know really can't hurt them.)

The 'reforms' undertaken by various Conservative health secretaries since 2010 have been a complete waste of time and money. They should be ended at once. And their reforms with them.

There are too many layers of middle management and they should be reduced by 50 per cent; what you need are doctors and nurses. Frontline NHS workers work incredibly hard in almost warlike conditions. Help them. Pay them. Properly. My £1 trillion a week budget should cover it. And on the flipside, as outlined earlier, I would ensure that all government ministers' pay is tied to that of nurses for the next hundred years.

The final key plank of my NHS manifesto is inspired by real-life stories on the healthcare front line. I know that an esteemed human named Adam Kay has made great waves by disseminating tales from his life as a doctor (and then getting Ben Whishaw to re-enact them charismatically on TV), and what makes Adam's account so gripping is its veracity. Being a responsible, sober-minded interstellar politician, when I arrived on Earth I similarly wanted to ground myself in the facts. So I immediately took it upon myself to learn about this incredible 'NHS' thing that everyone was banging on about. During the 2017 general election campaign I spoke to GPs and surgeons to find out what was going on and what changes were desperately needed. In the course of my research I made a discovery of shock and horror which I was only too happy to share with the audience for the Maidenhead hustings at the Oakley Court Hotel, and which I shall now recount for you too, dear reader. Strap in, because it may change the way you view your own species. It certainly inspired my most brilliant health policy of all: that **people should never ever be made to pay for any service they receive from the NHS, but when their treatment is the result**

of a self-inflicted and avoidable injury, I suggest that they are told what it would have cost if they did have to pay. How did I reach this conclusion? Well, I'm assuming that you must be a mature soul to be reading this book, so I'll tell you the story.

Not a million miles away from where you are right now there is an NHS Accident & Emergency unit, which one day in the 2010s was visited by a certain gentleman, who walked in complaining of having a permanent erection. This is true. When it was his turn to be seen, a doctor approached the man and she asked him, 'What happened?' To which he replied, 'I was at a party. And we were all, y'know, injecting crystal meth into our cocks. You know.' And she said, '*What*? No one does that.' And he said, 'Yes, well I did, and now it won't go down.' And the doctor explained, 'Well, we'll need to inject you and get rid of all the deoxygenated blood.' But he didn't like the idea of any more needles being inserted into his penis (even though he'd started it), and he wouldn't let the doctor touch it. She tried to convince him, stressing that he needed to be operated on because 'If we don't touch it, it will go black and die.' But he still refused, and you know what? It went black and died. This was a Saturday night in A&E. In the end he had to have a prosthetic cock fitted. On the NHS. Now I'm not saying he shouldn't have one. Of course he should. I'm just saying that sometimes you humans need to take a look at yourselves.

At this point I should like to make clear that I agree wholeheartedly with the doctor in the story, and I have a catchy slogan to help humans and all other intergalactic species, should you find yourself at a narcotic-fuelled party: 'JUST SAY NO... to injecting your reproductive organs with Class A drugs and ignoring the advice of healthcare professionals.'

Still, while individuals need to take a bit more responsibility, my major beef is with government ministers, and if the National Health Service isn't protected from all attempts at creeping privatisation, I will not hesitate to fire my miniaturising laser at the head of the current Secretary of State, and at the genitals of Matt Hancock. (I appreciate that at the time of publication Mr Hancock will have been without the Health brief for a fair while, but I am a politician after all, and zapping his little willy is sure to be a cast-iron vote winner.)

Any Other Policies?

Oh alright. I'll throw in free broadband as well.

Part Six

Prime Binister's Question Time

Part Six

Prime Time and Question Time

Since I first landed on Earth in 2017, a number of humans have seen fit to interview me about a range of topics on your planet and mine. I am almost always very happy to agree, unless it is for a particularly questionable platform, such as Russia Today or *Loose Women*. Here for your pleasure are transcripts from some of my favourite conversations so far during my election campaigning. *Frost/Nixon*, eat your internal fluid pumping organ out.

Do you think that Brexit is plunging Britain into a *Mad Max* dystopia? (Claire)

Not at all. Any space warrior with a cursory knowledge of human culture knows that the hellscape of *Mad Max: Fury Road* is a better comparison. The original is far too mild.

How will you distinguish yourself from the mainstream parties? (Martini Seltzermayr)

Well there's the bin for starters.

Where do you stand on skateboards? (Ian Payne)

I confess I am not an expert, but I believe one foot at each end is the standard procedure.

Hi, your Binificence, how would you solve world hunger? (Anthony Ryan)

Blimey. The evil solution to this is fewer people, but that's not my style. So how about fairer prices, smarter farming and a minimum price for fast-food joints selling hideous-quality meat? I can also drop you off a cruiser-load of space sludge. It's nutritious but tastes awful.

Hello O Great One, what the hell is going on in general with everything? (JTS)

Ah, you must be a Liberal Democrat.

Why do burgers come in packs of four or eight, but burger buns come in packs of six? What's that all about? (Aidan Diabolik)

Bill Gates innit.

Let's look at one of your more controversial policies: speaker phones on public transport to be banned. Offenders forced to watch the movie version of *Cats* every day for a year.' Does that include the James Corden bits and if so, does that not amount to a torture that Amnesty International might campaign against? (*NME*)

Yes it does. And yes it does.

Could you clarify what, in your view, would be a more sensible position for the hand-dryer in the gents' toilet at the Crown & Treaty, Uxbridge, and how it would differ from its current position? (Tomasz Oryński)

AWAY FROM THE URINALS. IT'S MADNESS. SHEER MADNESS.

Given the perilous state the UK finds itself in, with both Covid and Brexit wreaking havoc on the economy, my question is… who was the best Batman? West, Keaton, Kilmer, Clooney, Bale, Affleck, Pattinson? (Gizmo)

West. By a landslide.

Would you rather fight one horse-sized duck or 100 duck-sized horses? (Jack Pottinger)

I'll take on all 101. Remember, I've got the lasers.

What's your favourite cheese? (Deb)

Galaxeedam. It's the cheese with the wormholes.

Can we get more Greggs in central London? (Thom Marsh)

I don't know, can you? I'm genuinely keen to know if it's possible.

What's the best sherry for a trifle? (Mike Price)

In-date.

London is renowned as a global city with an international out-look, but this view is at risk due to Brexit. Can you pledge to make London the world's first City in the Sky, like Cloudbase off Captain Scarlet? And could you do it in your first term, please? (Sid Boggle)

This sounds suspiciously like a Boris project. Cities in the sky? Airports in the sea? You humans are mad.

How do we escape the mire of post-fact discourse in the early twenty-first century, and does the reintroduction of Ceefax have a role to play? (Dennis Kavanagh)

Spaceships. And YES!

When is the best time of year to lay turf? (Mark Cox)

Daytime.

Should pineapple be on pizza? (Liam Mason)

Only in Hawaii.

Mid-Devon District Council still haven't replaced our blue composting food caddy pinched five weeks ago. How would you stop the scourge? (Andrew Pitcher)

What a bunch of bastards. I'd message an intergalactic novelty politician about it.

In the interests of shifting the Overton Window to the left, would you consider advocating for dismantling industrial society? (Mitchell Broadbent)

Maybe, if I'm in the mood. I might remantle it the next day though.

Is your title hereditary or did you earn it for good works on this planet or any other? (Valleeblanche)

The domain was free.

Would you legislate to stop students learning trigonometry and outsource it to our superior alien overlords? It's a bit of a hassle. (Fin L)

Whaaaaat? You humans just do it on a calculator anyway! Such a lazy species.

How much for you to enter the marathon? (Russell Howe)

I'll do it for the return of Ceefax and a UHD *Lovejoy* box set.

How many roads must a man walk down? (Country Vince)

Wait till it's windy and you'll have your answer.

Opinions on the Falklands? (Twitta Enemy Number 1)

I'm sure there are.

Where do you stand on potentially bringing back dinosaurs and displaying them in a theme park setting? (Mike)

Health and safety nightmare, Mike.

Count Binface vs the *NME*

The following questions were put to me by that great journalistic organ the *NME*, across Earth years 2017 and 2021.

What's the first song you remember hearing?

I suppose it'd have to be a nursery rhyme when I was a young space warrior growing up. It goes like this: 'Twinkle twinkle huge quasar, please don't eat our local star.'

What song makes you cry?

See above.

What's the song you can no longer listen to?

'Maggie May', by Rod Stewart. I have no quarrel with the content of the song or with the husky knight himself, Sir Rod. But the mere title conjures the twin phantoms of a pair of British Prime Ministers with chequered records, so I tend to give this track a wide berth.

What song would you like to be played at your funeral?

This is a bit of a morbid question but if I must answer it then I'll plump for 'My Sweet Lord' by George Harrison. It nods to my lordly past, contains a contemplative tone, and features a member of the Fab Four, which is crucial because in my experience any list of favourite Earth songs lacking a Beatle is simply uncon-scionable. I also like 'He's So Fine' by the Chiffons, but this is entirely unconnected.

What's the first album you bought?

When I first visited Earth I was a bit homesick for the Sigma Quadrant and I wanted something to remind me of home, so I purchased a copy of *Stars* by Simply Red. I felt more homesick after that.

What's the first gig you went to?

On Earth I suppose it would have to be Sleaford Mods, a British band whom I introduced on stage at Glastonbury 2017. I was impressed by their pulsing rhythms and by the way that Jason and Andrew don't mince their words about the state of your nation. The crowd and the Park Stage setting were also spot on.

What song do you listen to before a political rally?

Without question, it has to be 'The Touch' by Stan Bush. Why you Earthlings didn't put this on the Voyager gold disc is beyond me. It's the quintessence of 1980s power rock from your solar system and I like to listen to it before any keynote speech or rally. If you have an important event coming up in your life I suggest you do the same. It will make you feel eight feet tall. (Having a bin for a head also has this effect.)

What song do you do at karaoke?

I'm a recent convert to the ways of karaoke because we don't have this in hyperspace, but I like it so much I've recently installed a system on my mothership. Anyone found to be tone deaf is blasted out of the airlock, so it's tremendous fun. My go-to track is 'Camouflage' by Stan Ridgway. It combines a fascinating lyric with a stonking chorus. What's more, it's a long song, so I get to hog the machine.

Part Seven

Predictions

As I mentioned in Part Two, I used to be the proud owner of a time machine until I got a little worse for wear one night and left it somewhere in the Asteroid Field of Fnor. Misplacing it still rankles. And the fact that the only thing I'd need in order to find it again is a time machine *really* stings. Be that as it may, having had some enjoyable travels through the past and the future, I still remember a good few nuggets of information about events which, as you read this, are yet to come to pass. Most of them aren't related to Earth, obviously, but I do know a fair bit about your planet's fate. So, as part of the public service element of this book, allow me to share some tasty morsels to whet your appetite for what the rest of the twenty-first century has in store for you guys. Hold onto your lids, humans. It's going to be quite a ride.

The 2020s

Sir Chris Whitty will leave the medical profession for a new, happier life in the children's playground industry, enjoying great success with his start-up company, Next Slide Please.

Melania Trump will be freed.

The Liberal Democrats will make a statement on the economy. I mention this simply because otherwise it won't be reported.

Owing to Brexit-related food shortages, the United Kingdom will become forced to rely on products for which there is a surplus, leading to a new national diet based on Bovril and Pot Noodles. Residents of Glasgow will see an upturn in health.

Meanwhile, in 2026, on the tenth anniversary of the EU referendum, the number of reasons given by the *Daily Mail* as to why 'whinging Remoaners' are to blame for Brexit being a disaster will hit 350 million a week.

After the success of elimination shows based on such skills as baking, sewing, spelling and pottery, in 2026 the new big hit series is Channel 4's *The Great British Jetwash the Patio*.

Count Binface will not use his Leviathan-class mother ship as a laser manufacturing centre in your solar system (which would, incidentally, allow him to avoid the punitive tax system of the Delta Quadrant). Count Binface's business interests are entirely principled, fair and above board. He cannot emphasise this enough.

In 2029, long since removed from office as Culture Secretary, Nadine Dorries will apply to be a panellist on *Loose Women*. She will fail.

Matt Hancock will take new jobs, as a non-executive director at both Bisto and Network Rail.

The Climate Irony Riots will begin, when citizens realise that politicians have so badly fucked things up that people can't afford to heat their homes while the entire planet is burning to a crisp.

The One Show will be indicted for crimes against humanity, with Matt Baker standing trial at the ICC in The Hague. His laudable work presenting *Countryfile* will not be enough to save him.

There's good news as the British population is invited to come forward for their hundredth Covid booster jab. There's less good news when scientists announce that the Omega variant has developed opposable thumbs.

Bitcoin will be found to be self-aware and to have been investing in itself. Nobody will know what this means. The fact that Bitcoin has also been investing in research and development for a series of cybernetic organisms, with living tissue over a metal endoskeleton, will not be discovered until much later.

In the media industry, a leaked report will blow open a huge scandal regarding the inaccuracy of television ratings, which are the cornerstone of commissioning decisions. During Ratingsgate, it will be revealed that Russians have hacked the computers that calculate ratings, inflating the figures for shows such as *The Apprentice* and *Sunday Brunch*, thus warping TV executives' ideas about what is popular with viewers. True figures will emerge proving that *Loose Men with Vernon Kay* is in fact watched by no one at all.

The 2030s

On their new Summer Sports channel, Sky TV will show wall-to-wall coverage of England's triumphant cricket team, but after complaints they will agree to show highlights of the men's team as well.

Will Smith will win a second Oscar for the movie *Slaps Stick*, his new biopic detailing the story of his assault on Chris Rock and how the disgrace stuck.

The 2032 Winter Olympics will be awarded to Antarctica, as the last cold place left.

The 2036 Summer Olympics will be awarded to Antarctica.

Years after the death of the great Sir David Attenborough, the BBC Natural History Unit will make a big misstep with their succession planning by hiring David Moyes. After this unhappy interregnum, harmony will be restored when the BBC appoints Zig and Zag to front *Blue Planet 5* (aka *Blue Planet: Endgame*).

The Communist Party will remain in power in China. Clearly I'm sticking my neck out here, which is something that I would strongly advise their internal opponents not to do.

In 2034 Bob Geldof will announce his new anniversary charity single 'Band Aid 50 – Do They Still Not Know it's Christmas?' Ethiopia will respond by immediately declaring war on Europe, the crisis ending only when Geldof is handed over as a blood sacrifice.

After the North Pole finally melts, a change will be forced to the traditional Christmas myth, with Father Christmas relocating to the Costa del Sol. The Spanish postal system will subsequently grind to a halt after the world's children write letters to him at his new address in Malaga. Meanwhile, after decades of persistent and worsening redness, Rudolph's nose will be removed by doctors as a precaution.

Ambitious billionaire Elon Musk will take advantage of fluctuating property prices by buying the whole of Doncaster. He will then raze it to the ground and build a brick-by-brick replica of central London in the north of England, promising: 'No hipsters'. He will make a lot of money.

Former Prime Minister Boris Johnson will take a new job as life chairman of the Wellcome Trust, throwing doubt on the veracity of both words in the institution's name.

To compensate for a lack of fuel duty by the growth in electric cars, tolls will be introduced on all roads except those in Milton Keynes, where you will only have to pay to leave.

The iPhone 30 will be banned from sale after it is discovered that users can launch targeted airstrikes from a new app. The product will earn a reprieve after Apple points out in court that the battery never lasts long enough to cause any damage.

The 2040s

With his film career on the skids again, septuagenarian Will Smith will shock the world by slapping Russell Brand at the Oscars after Brand makes an ill-judged joke. This time, unlike 2022, Smith will decide that he should leave the auditorium, until he is persuaded by the thousands present to stay and receive a standing ovation.

In 2041, Nadine Dorries will break the record for failed attempts to get on *Loose Women*.

After reports of an unemployed rambler being shot on the Balmoral estate, twenty-five-year-old Prince Louis will give a notorious *Newsnight* interview in which he defends the incident as 'a straightforward shooting weekend'.

Human astronauts will find life on Mars, reporting that it is primitive and unintelligent. The Martian life forms will feel precisely the same way.

Mark Zuckerberg will announce that the Metaverse is closed after Nick Clegg is revealed as the only member. Zuckerberg will come clean and admit that even he didn't join it for this reason.

When they are back in power, the Conservatives will make a push to privatise what's left of the BBC. Concerns will be raised about the shortlist of would-be buyers, including P&O Ferries, Matt Hancock's sister, a cryogenically preserved Richard Branson and the Gulf state of Qatar. Disaster will be averted when they are diverted to bid for Channel 5 instead.

Someone will marry their iPhone 40. Later it will turn out that the groom is still seeing his iPhone 20 on the side.

The big TV hit of 2043 will be a new, nostalgia-infused reality dating show in which lovelorn singletons are encouraged to find their soulmate, but with a twist – they must spend several weeks going on well-chosen dates at restaurants, galleries and national parks, at all times keeping their clothes on. The last eligible bachelor to send a dick pic to a woman wins. Called *Clothed Attraction*, the format will be syndicated to every country on Earth.

The United Kingdom will receive a shock when the Dorset Independence Party surprisingly wins a referendum to leave the union. Their victory will be based upon the Nicola Sturgeon play-book of 'Blame the Tories'. Given that every single Dorset MP is a Tory, it's a surprising but brilliant tactic.

At the sprightly age of 100, Paul McCartney will headline the 2042 Glastonbury Festival.

By the end of the decade, Count Binface will have secured control of Earth, all his policies will be enacted and planet Earth will be saved.

Disneyland will be overtaken in popularity by Lovelovejoyworld – a new theme park dedicated to *Lovejoy*, featuring a lovely antique teacup ride, a giant leather jacket market (complete with a faux-leather jackfruit hide clothing range for vegan fans), leisurely country drives in vintage open-top cars, and a giant interactive *Homes under the Hammer* exhibit.

The 2050s

The glorious Binface revolution will be halted in 2051 when an aged and decrepit Boris Johnson will become Prime Minister again with a landslide general election victory, all nineteen million of his votes coming from his direct descendants, a critical mass of whom will by that time have reached voting age.

All this is just for starters. I won't tell you more. I don't want to spoil the surprise. But it will happen. Maybe not all of it in your universe. But it'll happen.

Part Eight

A New Hope

Well, there you go. That's your lot. There's plenty more I could tell you about how to save your little planet and its even littler politics, but I've got to keep some of my wisdom in my back holster. Otherwise the 'mainstream' parties will start pilfering all my new ideas before the next election, and I'll have less material for the inevitable sequel to this smash hit book (which I'm thinking of calling *The Thursday Electoral Murders Club*. That's got a nice ring to it.)

Some sniffy political commentators on Earth will scoff at my mission to enter Parliament. They will call it a sideshow, a joke, a nonsense, and their co-conspirators in the bookshop industry (or 'Big Bookshop') may go so far as to place this book in the 'humour' section, as opposed to the political theory section where it clearly belongs. But I shall close my treatise by sounding a warning note to any sceptical voices who don't rate my chances of becoming first an MP and then PM. All you have to do is think back to the year 2016, when there was another democratic outpouring for an outsider candidate, whose legend lives on loudly in the present day.

The story goes like this. The United Kingdom had done something wonderful and built a brand new polar research vessel to explore the mysteries of Antarctica. And then they did something even more wonderful: they gave humans the opportunity to name it. Several people came up with suggestions, most notably a BBC Jersey presenter called James Hand who, despite the handicap of being a local radio DJ, did something of importance. In one small step for a man, and one giant leap for *Good Morning Jersey*, James suggested that the ship should be dubbed 'Boaty McBoatface', a moniker that quickly caught on and trounced all opposition to win the poll.

But as you must surely know, in a scandal from which planet Earth has yet fully to recover, there was no happy ending. The chance to give the new ship its wonderful, democratically chosen name was spurned by the Conservative government. Looking back now, we can see that this is an administration which during its time in office since 2010 oversaw punishing austerity, a catastrophic Brexit deal and a woefully mismanaged approach to a pandemic, and in its catalogue of heinous errors the Boaty decision is right up there. How could the bastards claim that the 2016 EU referendum was a binding vote while being simultaneously willing to ride roughshod over democracy like this? – I hear you cry. And you'd be right to cry. Because instead of following the people's will, science minister Jo Johnson* opted to name the new Royal Research Ship the *Sir David Attenborough* instead, deigning to christen one of the icebreaker's remotely controlled

---

* Very much the Waluigi to Boris Johnson's Wario.

submersibles Boaty McBoatface. It was a cop-out. An outrageously feeble cop-out. I should emphasise I have nothing whatsoever against the great Sir David, who didn't ask to be involved in this scandal, but it's not even like he came second in this election. He finished in fifth place, 495 votes behind the honourable suggestion, 'It's Bloody Cold Here'.

But the big news was Boaty, and he has since entered the general galactic lexicon as a phrase, a meme, and indeed a warning shot to overbearing politicians. Now, dear reader, dear voter, I am calling upon you to join with me and, at the next election, help me avenge Mr McBoatface. For I am the Binny McBinface of democratic politics and it is high time to teach the establishment a lesson it will never forget – that Parliament has become so ridiculous that the ridiculous candidate is the only sane choice on the menu. Join me and together we will rule the galaxy as overlord and subject. (I'll do the ruling. You can just sit back and chill.)

Whoever you vote for, do vote whenever you get the chance. Democracy is a rare and amazing thing, and take it from me, not many planets have it. Politicians are your servants, and election day is the special moment when you can give them a pat on the back, from either your hand or a cow, depending on whether they're any good.

And as for the type of voter I want to attract, I'm aiming to pinpoint that part of the electorate that happens to think that the Conservatives, Labour, Liberal Democrats, SNP and Greens are all a bit shit. If I can attract them, I reckon I'm in with an above average chance of one day seizing power.

So then. Have I convinced you? I will end with a call to action. If you support me and want to see me take control of the British Parliament and the wider Earth, simply place your bin outside your home at some point this week or next. This will be unquestionable evidence of your fealty to me, and it will have the corridors of Westminster quaking in their sleazy boots.

It is time for planet Earth to take out the trash. To celebrate Bindependence Day. To make its votes Count. To elect Count Binface.

Peace and love(joy).
CB x

Part Nine

A Promise Kept

Count Binface's favourite recipe

Take one populist politician known for deflection, adultery and incompetence.

Place in a tin pot.

Steam slowly above a boiling water bath for twelve weeks.

Remove and then grill lightly, using a forensic interviewer (must not, repeat NOT, be from the Metropolitan Police or this will have no effect).

Sear the testicles using a Class A laser. Or if you don't have one of those (yet), a blowtorch will do the job fine.

Remove any remaining tufts of blond hair.

Pour over a generous glug of olive oil. Then tar and feather.

Place in The London Dungeon, inside a custom-made glass-walled room as their new exhibit.

Over a specially-installed speaker system, play on a never-ending loop the sound of a voice reading out the names of every single human impacted adversely by the life and career of the politician. (For maximum excruciation, book Theresa May for the voiceover gig.)

Allow five Earth years, and then watch as the leader slowly bastes himself in the salt-water of his own tears.

That's it.

NB. Do not eat. That is a fate too good for him.

This recipe is best washed down with a hard-hitting drink. My personal favourite is a Large Hadron Colada, but whatever's your poison.

Thanks

The lion's share of the research for this book was carried out by myself, with assistance from my loyal lieutenant General Waste and my computer, Barry. However, to help fine-tune my account of the minutiae of Earth politics, I would like to pay tribute to a small but plucky band of human support staff. Thank you to the following: my special adviser Jon Harvey for his occasionally useful input; researchers Tom Walker and Laura Major for their diligent analysis; associates Neil and Schad for their auxiliary aid; the sage counsel of Stan, Julia Wyatt and Kate Haldane; the wonderful support of Sarah Daykin and Lizzie Daykin; the enthusiasm of Rowan Harkin and Peggy; Professor Stephen Harrison for his linguistic prowess (which rivals my own) and the brilliance of Katy Follain and all the staff at Quercus Books.

And a final thanks once more to all the beautiful human beings who have voted for me so far in UK elections. This is not the end. It is not even the beginning of the end. But it is the end of the beginning.

COUNT BINFACE WILL RETURN